Written by: Mark Rushall

Acknowledgements

Though Ryan Wriggleback is an imaginary coach, all his stories, hints and tips are real, and come from hard-earned lessons: some are mine, some are my sailing and coaching partners', and some we have been subjected to by our athletes! A huge thank you is due to all, especially Chips Howarth, Adam May, Mike Austen, and Liz Rushall.

Photo Credits

Melges 24: Fiona Brown; Musto Skiff: Paul Manning; Mumm 30: Mike Austen; Fireball: fotoboat; RIB: Pix-u; Classroom debrief: Richard Langdon/Skandia Team GBR. All other photos by Mark Rushall.

www.rya.org.uk

Royal Yachting Association

RYA House, Ensign Way, Hamble, Southampton SO31 4YA
Tel: 0845 345 0400 Fax: 0845 345 0329
email: publications@rya.org.uk website: www.rya.org.uk

ISBN: 978-1-905104-21-5

A CIP record of this book is available from the British Library.

Note:
While all reasonable care has been taken in the preparation of this book, the publisher takes no responsibility for the use of the methods or products or contracts described in the book.

Cover design: Pete Galvin
Typeset: Creativebyte
Illustrations: Pete Galvin
Proof-reading and indexing: Alan Thatcher
Printed in China through: World Print

Ring 0845 345 0400 for a copy of our Publications Catalogue.

Totally Chlorine
Free

Sustainable
Forests

Contents

Foreword

Ryan Wriggleback is the alter ego of one of the best tactical sailors and coaches in the world, namely Mark Rushall.

Through the eyes of Ryan, 'Tactics' manages to explain the complexities of sailboat tactics in a fun and informative way. Racing tactics are both a science and an art and our friend Ryan perfectly captures this balance to allow sailors of all skill levels to understand, improve and even coach tactical sailing to a higher level.

Like no other sport, sailing tests both your physical and mental ability, and with so many tactical decisions needing to be made throughout a race, it is no wonder sailing has been described as 'waterborne chess'. The cerebral side of our sport can be the most challenging, frustrating and rewarding aspect of sailing and a greater understanding will only enhance every race we sail.

This book has come about from years of sailing and coaching at the highest level by an extremely analytical person. Mark, a qualified Physics teacher, is one of those annoying people who learnt from every sailing/coaching experience and has built an extensive memory bank of tactical scenarios and understanding.

I first met Mark at a Lark National Championships many years ago (that he won with straight firsts in a fleet of ninety boats) and you could spot his boat as it was always on the lifted tack, but never appeared vulnerable when the next shift arrived. In the final shake down to the first mark, his boat was always 'safe', inevitably popping out in the front bunch. His regatta was sailed with a superior tactical performance that led to his success.

We are all lucky enough to gain from this experience and knowledge, and via Ryan, we are guided through in a unique style that will improve our sailing.

Please read, enjoy, learn and when you see the improvements in your tactical thinking on the race course, remember to give a 'nod' to your tactic super coach, Ryan Wriggleback.

Introduction
What wins sailboat races?

Nothing in sailboat racing is certain. But teams that regularly win would probably agree that they have an advantage over their competitors in at least some of the following categories:

BOAT SPEED
- equipment
- rig set-up
- trim
- technique
- personal fitness

BOAT HANDLING
- standard manoeuvres
- mark-rounding manoeuvres
- starting manoeuvres
- close company manoeuvres

TACTICS
- weather
- tide
- coastal effects
- strategy
- tactics
- rules

Introduction

*"Ryan Wriggleback, our resident coach, compares racing a sailboat to baking a cake: "To bake a good cake you have to start with the right ingredients. If you have no flour, you can't put it right by adding more eggs, even if they are extra large free range! You can't rely on **Tactics** alone to win your club race: your speed through the water has to be on the same level as the boats you are trying to beat. If you need a good tack and a quick duck off the start line to cross the rest of the fleet to the favoured side, your boat handling has to be up to the job. To appreciate this you only have to speak to Olympic medallists to understand just how fanatical they are about gaining an extra millimetre: the speed enables them to sail a tactically correct, conservative race. Average speed gives mediocre results, or encourages risky tactics: they sometimes work, but not consistently.*

*"To make **Tactics** win races, boat speed and boat handling have to be as good as the best. Otherwise all you get is a really nice omelette!*

"One of the assumptions in this book is that our boat handling and boat speed are at least as good as the boats in our race."

As Ryan hints, good boat speed and boat handling skills - general and class specific - increase the effectiveness of both large and small scale tactics. Below are some questions we should ask ourselves: All need out-of-race practice, and all vary with wave and wind speed conditions.

- What are the most effective upwind acceleration techniques? How long does it take to get from a controlled stall to full speed in the range of wind and range conditions?

- How far advanced do we have to be to make a lee bow tack successful?

- Can we perform a controlled duck, exiting at maximum speed with bow just clear of the other boat's stern?

- How much ground does a tack lose… or two quick tacks, in each condition?

- What are the techniques for gaining height while losing minimum speed? And trading height to move forward on the boats around?

- What line gives the "perfect" leeward mark rounding, exiting close hauled, inches from the mark, at maximum speed?

- How close can we swing our bow clear across the transom of the boat ahead?

- In which direction and how far does the wind shadow extend downwind?

Tactics or strategy?

The broader term of **Tactics** covers all aspects of the positioning of our boat around the race course. For simplicity we divide this up into strategy (the route we take to get there quickly) and tactics (how we get there, dealing with the other boats, and instantaneous changes).

Part 1 of this book describes the main environmental variables - "natural assets"- which might affect our race course, suggesting a winning strategy for each.

Part 2 discusses ways to establish which natural assets apply on the day, including use of the race compass, and how to prioritise these assets to build the strategy. This includes the pre-start period.

Part 3 discusses each part of the race in detail, looking at specific tactics for each part of the race.

Using the examples

In an attempt to champion equality in sailing, we have indiscriminately changed the gender of the sailors of the main contenders in the diagrams: "Outstanding Orange", "Mediocre Mauve", and "Shocking Pink" throughout the book.

The diagrams generally assume that the average wind direction blows from the top of the page. We describe wind shifts as "right" or "left" according to the direction of movement looking upwind. Thus a "right shift" means that the wind direction has moved clockwise, i.e. compass numbers have increased. (Known as a "veer" in proper yacht club bars.) A "left shift" refers to an anticlockwise movement, and smaller compass numbers (a "back").

We refer to the "starboard" and "port" end of the line, though Ryan does occasionally lapse into "committee boat" and "pin." There is a glossary at the end of the book aimed at demystifying any other sailing jargon we have unwittingly included in the book.

Key to Symbols used in illustrations throughout this book.

Boat path

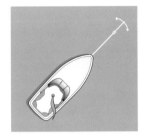

Committee boat

Mark and start line

Sailing wind

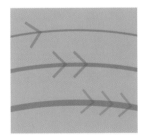

Tide strength

Wind

Layline/track to next mark

Tide

Coach

Part 1: Setting the scene
INTRODUCTION: Why bother with a strategy?

"Ryan Wriggleback is the first to peel onto port tack, having made a conservative start near the port end of the line. Ducking three transoms, he continues on port for five minutes. He reacts to a five-degree port header by tacking back onto starboard. Two boats continue on port tack toward the starboard lay line. The wind continues to lift on starboard, giving Ryan an advantage over the majority of the fleet, now to leeward. Ryan flicks back onto port, narrowing the gap on the boats to windward. Some are now on starboard and look to be right on the layline, slightly ahead.

"Ryan tacks back onto starboard, below but bow-forward of the leaders, some 3 boats' lengths below the layline. 'Land's moving right' calls Ryan's crew, who has taken a transit from the windward mark to the shore. 'Tide's taking us up there, ease a touch' is the reply.

"Ryan rounds the mark first, comfortably ahead of the pack of boats on the left of the course, who missed the persistent right hand shift. The boats on the layline misjudged the tide and have reached down to fall in line behind his transom."

Another lucky beat: or good strategy? Here is Ryan's observation:

- *" We tracked the wind direction for the half hour before the start, and found that it was shifting back and forth through five to ten degrees. The average wind heading moved progressively right, which matched this morning's forecast.*
- *"We monitored the tide at the pin end: it was flowing from left to right and slightly over the line. Our tidal atlas indicated that this would continue for several hours.*
- *"Though the line was very port biased when we checked it, we decided to start in a gap some way from the pin so we could tack onto port on the first shift. We picked up a safe transit, as we were concerned that the tide might take us over the line. I'm surprised that the boats we ducked weren't OCS!"*

Ryan clearly used the time available before the race's starting sequence to build a picture of the race conditions. Using this picture helped him to plan the start, his first beat, and react instinctively to wind, tide, and other boats.

Though the plan will develop during the race - or even the leg - as situations change, the race and leg strategy revolves around external factors, i.e. those not affected by racing boats. This section of the book focuses on some of the major "natural assets" we are likely to experience, and suggests an ideal strategy for each one. We'll also discuss how our sailing style and objectives, and the state and type of regatta could affect our decision making.

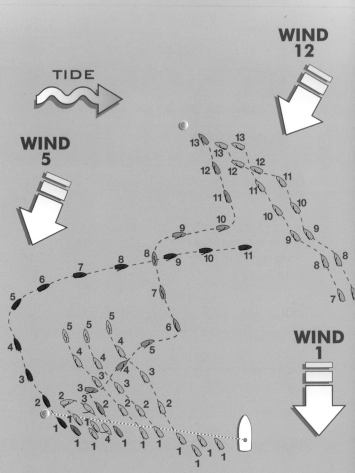

Natural assets: the strategic tools outlined

"Venue characteristics", "Gain features", "Natural assets"… These are all terms used to describe the meteorological, geographical and other external effects that affect the fastest way around the race course: the factors which determine our racing strategy at any time. This chapter identifies the major variables which affect our decisions around the race course, and suggests a winning strategy for each.

Four types of wind shift

"An understanding of the basic types of windshift, and how to deal with each, is one of the biggest steps towards building a race winning strategy. The compass is the best tool we have for identifying and analysing windshift patterns, we'll discuss the mechanics of using the race compass later in this section. First let's identify the different types of shift we might expect, and suggest a strategy for each."

Wind Features

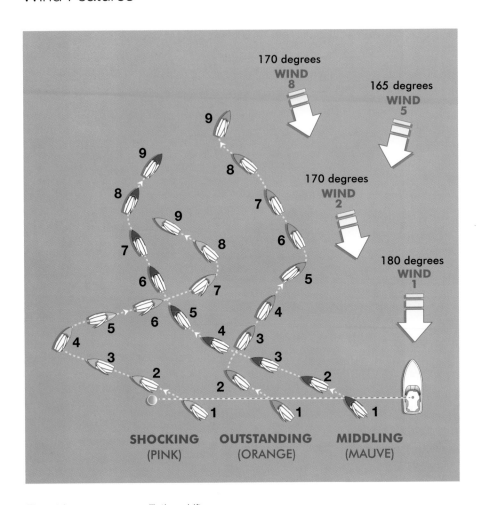

Fig 1.1 Instantaneous oscillating shifts

Oscillating shifts

The wind shifts back and forth around a mean. In this example the mean is 180 degrees (fig 1.1).

1. The boats start evenly, and just after the start at position 2, they are headed 15 degrees. The wind is now 15 degrees left of its mean. Orange tacks onto the lifted port tack. At position 5, orange is headed 25 degrees; the wind is now 10 degrees right of mean. Orange returns to the lifted starboard tack, and so on. By tacking in phase with the shifts, orange has sailed the shortest course. Pink has done precisely the opposite, and is left trailing, while mauve's "two-tack" strategy puts him on the gaining tack just 50% of the time.

 "On a lake the shifts hit us in the face: the jib backs, it's time to tack! On open water the shifts tend to arrive more gradually: the optimum time to tack is when we are headed to below the average course for that tack."

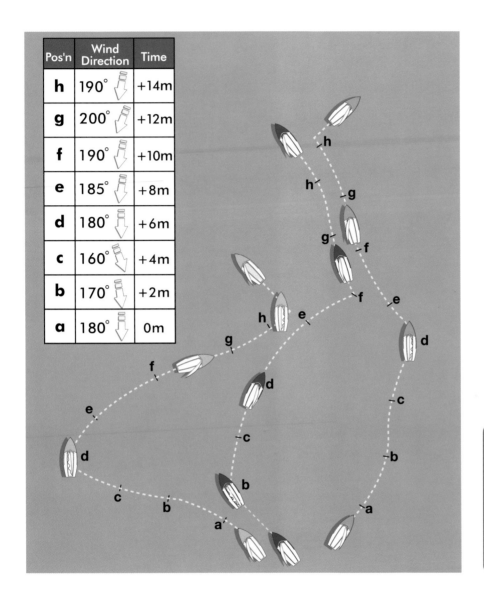

Pos'n	Wind Direction	Time
h	190°	+14m
g	200°	+12m
f	190°	+10m
e	185°	+8m
d	180°	+6m
c	160°	+4m
b	170°	+2m
a	180°	0m

COACH TOP TIP

"The winning strategy in oscillating conditions is: tack on the headers; in swinging conditions, tack when headed below the mean!"

Fig 1.2 *Swinging oscillating shifts*

Swinging oscillating shifts

Now the wind is swinging progressively between 160 degrees and 200 degrees (fig 1.2). Again the boats start with the wind at its mean direction of 180 degrees. Orange, starting on port tack, is initially lifted as the wind swings to its extreme left direction of 160, and then headed as it moves into its right hand phase. As soon as the wind direction is right of the 180 degree mean, orange tacks, and the process repeats on starboard tack. Orange makes best use of the swinging oscillating shifts by tacking whenever she's headed below her mean heading for each tack. Pink couldn't have got it more wrong if she had tried, with Mauve somewhere in between!

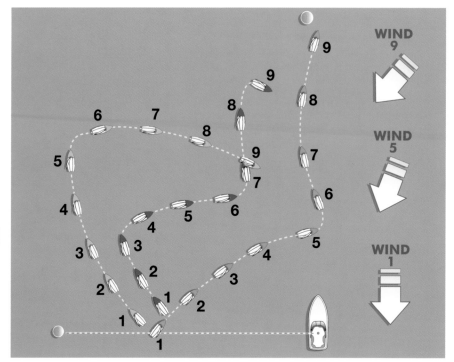

Fig 1.3 *Persistent right hand shift*

Persistent shift

Over a period of time, the wind persistently moves in one direction (fig 1.3).

Orange sails towards the new wind direction first. He spends half of the beat being progressively headed, but sails a much shorter course than pink.

 "If we are more used to oscillating conditions, it does feel strange to keep sailing into the header. But if we know that the wind is going to keep moving one way, the fast track is to do just that."

In the Northern Hemisphere, a sea breeze will often swing persistently to the right as the afternoon passes. A persistent shift pattern may also be caused by an overall change in weather system, for example as a slow moving front moves through.

 "Now for another complication: what if we have an overall oscillating wind shift pattern but the wind is taking so long to track from furthest right to furthest left that we get to the windward mark before it swings back? This could easily happen on a short beat. If the wind is near its most extreme, and starts to shift right as we round the leeward mark, tacking on to the lifted starboard tack would be just as effective as Pink's strategy in fig 1.3! For the length of the beat, we'd have a persistent shift. However, depending on the phasing of the shifts, the wind could just as likely be moving persistently right on the second beat!"

We'll look at ways to identify this sort of situation in more detail in "Using the compass"(p41).

COACH TOP TIP

"The winning strategy for a persistent shift is: sail towards the new wind direction: if it's going right, go right!"

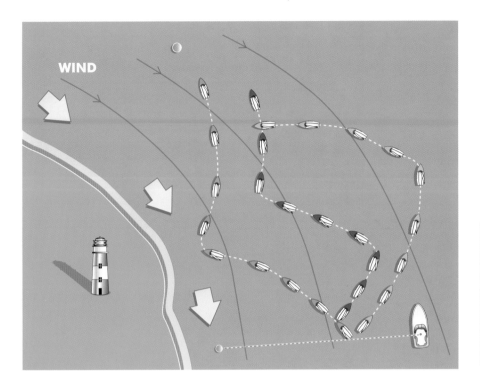

Fig 1.4 Wind bend

COACH TOP TIP

"The winning strategy in a wind bend is: sail towards the inside of the bend: in other words; "sail into the header!"

Wind bend

Wind direction is always affected by local topography. We typically find that the wind bends around a headland, or along a curving valley. In the Northern Hemisphere, the wind direction over a landscape with plenty of trees or buildings will be appreciably further left than the wind over the sea, while in the Southern Hemisphere it'll be further right. Therefore we'd expect to experience a wind bend when approaching the shore in an offshore breeze. (In an onshore wind we don't sail in the bend: it occurs over the land!)

There is a significant wind bend around the headland (fig 1.4). Outstanding Orange sails towards the inside of the bend, and sails 3 boat lengths less distance than Middling Mauve. Shocking Pink gets it all wrong again and sails another 3 boat lengths further.

"With a persistent shift the wind changes direction as time passes. With a bend, the direction varies with position on the course. Though the method for confirming each feature is different, on the beat the strategy is the same for each: we sail on the headed tack first."

Permanent shift

The permanent shift is every race officer's nightmare. The beat becomes a reach. Rubber boats drive all over the course at high speed waving red, green, and/or code flag "C". Eventually the fleet works out the new course and the race continues. The permanent shift is typically caused by a sea breeze replacing an offshore breeze, but could be caused by other weather changes.

It is virtually impossible to have a strategy for a permanent shift in an inshore race: however good our weather information is we can never be certain exactly when it will happen. All we can do is be aware (preparation) and watch for early signs of the shift coming (observation).

Real Life

Of course it's not that straightforward: often the day's conditions provide a combination of types of wind shifts. In Chapter 4: Using the Race Compass, we'll look at ways to spot wind shift patterns, and strategies for dealing with mixed conditions.

A couple of extra knots breeze (or "pressure" as it's known in sailboat racing circles) will give performance dinghies more upwind speed, while more pressure will give keelboats already sailing at displacement speed a narrower tacking angle. In both cases, as we'd expect, sailing in more wind will get us to the windward mark more quickly.

Variation in wind strength

"In light winds, we might experience 2 knots wind speed in one part of the course, and 4 knots in another. Boat speed will be significantly different: sailing in more pressure is obviously going to be important. In medium conditions, an extra two knots breeze may not be so critical, but we'd accept it if it was on offer!"

Wind breaks

Pressure is rarely constant across the race course. A lake surrounded by trees or buildings will have areas of calm behind the obstructions, with stronger bands where it funnels between them. The further away the obstructions are from the course, the less the effect. On a larger scale, an island to windward of the course can result in more pressure on one side of the course than the other, for example when sailing in the Berkley circle in San Francisco Bay, the more of the Golden Gate Bridge you can see around the island, the more wind you feel.

Acceleration/deceleration

When wind blows over a high cliff onto the water, as well as the expected light patch immediately behind the cliff, there may be more breeze where the deflected wind finally hits the water, and less further out to sea.

When the wind blows around a headland, as well as the expected bend, there is often more pressure where the breeze is compressed around the obstruction, with relative calm downwind and inshore of the point.

The darker ripples on the right are a clear indication of more breeze on that side of the course

Areas of more or less breeze can also move around or across the race course, often driven by the clouds. On a summer's day with patches of cumulus cloud passing over the course, the additional thermal "mixing" under the clear patches will give more wind (which is also likely to be *veered*) compared with the breeze under the clouds. However rain clouds have a different effect: the falling rain under the cloud initially pushes the air outward in all directions, causing a squall of strong breeze which lasts until all the air under the cloud is cooled by the falling rain.

Convergence/divergence

As we've discussed, in the Northern Hemisphere, the wind over the land is relatively backed compared with the wind over the sea. So, when the wind direction is near parallel to the coastline we may experience convergence or divergence, up to around 5 kilometres from the shore.

An increase in wind speed closer to the shore is caused by the backed wind over the land converging with the wind over the sea.

Reduced wind speed inshore is caused by the backed wind over the land diverging from the wind over the sea.

In both conditions there would be more wind on the left hand side of the course, looking upwind. (The effect would be reversed in the Southern Hemisphere). In the extreme example of sailing on a lake or wide river, we could experience one effect on the left shore, and the other on the right.

"There are plenty of reasons for pressure varying over the course. Sometimes the bands of pressure move, sometimes they hang around. Understanding the theory is all very well, you've got to look out for it as well. Practise identifying pressure from the telltale signs on the water: more white water; darker ripples; packs of boats to one side of the course moving faster, or cruising boats heeling more."

COACH TOP TIP

"The winning strategy in variable wind strength is: sail in more breeze!"

Preparing for wind features

Some successful racers appear simply to follow instinct, while others have a more structured approach to preparation and decision-making, and a logical explanation for what has happened. Both approaches win regattas.

"I believe that the instinctive approach is a result of learning through experience, especially as a young sailor. 'Natural' sailors rely on a subconscious memory of what was successful in similar conditions last year/decade/century. I always encourage my budding champions to develop and trust in a feel for what works in what conditions."

Every day at every venue has its own particular wind pattern. Identifying and understanding this pattern before the race will make those regatta winning decisions more straightforward. Later we'll look at some of the ways we can recognise these patterns ahead of the race.

Through this chapter we've looked at effects rather than causes. The recommended reading list (page 23) suggests titles which cover the background behind most of the natural assets discussed. In particular, note that most of the wind direction effects discussed in this chapter are reversed in the Southern Hemisphere.

But don't forget to check it out!

"Nothing in sailing is certain, particularly predictions of wind effects: strength and direction. Sailing at Lake Garda, the popular wisdom is that there is more wind near the cliffs, as the flow is compressed and funnels into the narrow part of the lake. But we have had days where there is a distinct light wind channel up to 100m from the shore. We have seen sailors following their coaches' instructions to the letter, only to sit and wallow as their competitors plane past just metres further off shore!

"However confident we are of our predictions, the only way to be sure is to get out there and try it out!"

In the distance at Lake Garda, the windsurfers enjoy the wind acceleration around the point, while further downwind towards the camera there is a channel of light wind and swirling gusts.

Water features

"If you think wind effects are complicated, try planning a beat across the various banks in the Eastern Solent just as the tide starts to turn! Even the "old salts" sometimes get it wrong. The tidal flow is at a different speed and a different direction at every location, and these variables are continuously changing with time!"

In the UK, we describe moving sea water as "tide", and river water as "current". To race, we want to know what is happening to the water we are actually sailing in: the stream within a metre or so of the surface. Which way is it flowing, how strongly, how does it vary over the course, and how will the situation change with time? This applies to all moving water, be it river current, tidal stream or surface wind-driven current. Knowledge of the most likely effects will help us to build a picture of the stream pattern, which can then be incorporated into our race strategy.

Common stream effects: Depth

The rate of flow of the water near the surface is affected by its depth. The layer of water nearer the bottom is slowed significantly through friction. Therefore, the further away from the bottom, the faster the flow. In deeper water, we'd expect the flow at the surface to be stronger, while in shallower water, the flow is weaker (fig 1.5). Usually this shallow water is found as we sail further inshore, but the same effect occurs over shallow banks further offshore.

Other factors may override this principle, for example where a large quantity of water is forced to flow over rather than round an obstruction, it accelerates. This often happens over a bar near a harbour entrance.

Bends

The water usually runs faster towards the outside of a bend in the channel (fig 1.5). This effect is often enhanced because over time, the faster moving water carves a deeper channel on the outside of the bend, allowing even stronger stream over the deeper channel on the outside!

Fig 1.5 *Stronger stream towards the outside of the bend, strongest in the deepest water.*

Bays and obstructions

Just as the wind accelerates around a headland, there is often more current around a point or an obstruction, with less, or even an eddy behind. This can apply to a whole bay, where the point at one end of the bay "shields" the bay from the current; or more locally to an individual point along a bank or coastline.

Turning tide

When the tide flows parallel with a coastline, it frequently turns first inshore. The main mass of water offshore takes longer to slow and reverse than the shallow water further inshore.

"Watch for this effect on moored boats: the inshore ones swing significantly earlier than those moored further offshore."

Effect on the sailing wind

Imagine we are sailing downwind in slack stream, with our speedometer reading 5 knots (through the water speed). While maintaining 5 knots through the water, our tactician finds us an area of 2 knots favourable stream. We are now travelling at 7 knots over the land, our GPS could confirm this. We'd feel 2 knots less wind: the stream carries us downwind, reducing our *"sailing wind"* correspondingly.

Conversely, if we sailed downwind at the same speed through the water, an adverse stream of 2 knots would slow our progress to 3 knots over the land, and increase the wind we feel by 2 knots. The stream changes the strength of the wind we sail in (sailing wind). A moored buoy or committee boat feels neither effect: the stream does not affect them, they feel and read the wind over the ground only.

When the stream is at an angle to the breeze, the angle of the sailing wind as well as its strength is affected (fig 1.6). The stream has a partial component in the same direction as the wind. Effectively, each boat is being pushed in the direction of the tidal arrow, which affects the wind it feels. The boats are pushed away from the wind; the sailing wind speed is therefore less than the true wind speed. The stream also has a component from right to left across the page. Blue, on port tack feels a lift. Pink, on starboard, feels a header. Red, who would be beam reaching on starboard if there were no stream, has been headed, while Grey, who would have been running on port gybe, is actually broad reaching on starboard. The point is that irrespective of which direction they are pointing, the sailing wind for each boat sailing on this piece of water is backed and is lighter than with the breeze which would be measured on the anchored boat. The stronger the stream, the bigger the effect on the sailing wind.

"Looking upwind, if the stream has a right to left component, the sailing wind will be shifted to the left. If left to right, to the right. If it has a component with the wind the sailing wind will be lighter than the ground wind, if against, it will be stronger."

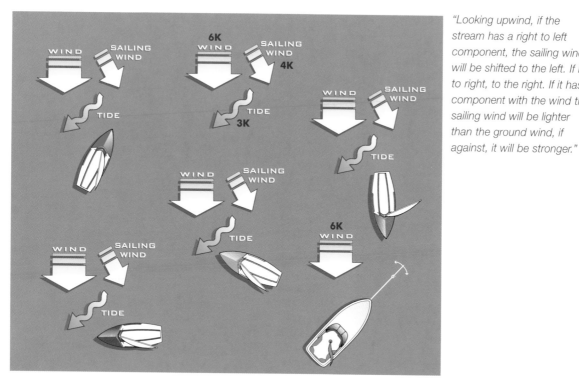

Fig 1.6 *The wind we sail in is affected by the tide, independently of the direction we are sailing. The wind on the anchored committee boat is not.*

Stream uniform across the course

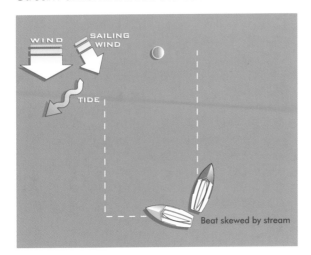

Fig 1.7 *Beat skewed by stream*

If the anchored committee boat uses its flag or wind instruments to lay the course, the combination of the port lift in sailing wind, and the stream pushing the boats to the left, will skew the beat considerably (fig 1.7). "Course features" (p21) suggests strategies for skewed courses.

Because it's so much harder to judge laylines in tide or current, it rarely pays to hit either one early if the stream is uniform. In fig 1.7, it's all too easy to be pushed to the left of the port layline. A port tack approach to the windward mark would result. The boats on the starboard layline are highly likely to have under laid the mark. They will be stacked up and moving slowly, leaving any port tack approachers little chance to tack inside!

COACH TOP TIP

"If the stream is uniform across the course, we can predict the way the stream will affect laylines, and plan the windward mark approach accordingly. Once on the final approach, a transit will confirm whether we are laying, (see p??) and ensure that we sail the direct course to the mark, rather than a great circle route".

Non uniform stream

When sailing closer to the shore, or in estuaries, harbours, or rivers, tidal strength and direction often vary with position and time. These multiple combinations lead to an infinite number of solutions.

If the stream direction is fairly constant over the course, but strength varies, we minimise time sailing against, and maximise time sailing with, the strongest current, using the common effects described above. Take the classic situation of a beat against the tide, when there is slacker water (or sometimes even helpful stream) close inshore, but strong adverse stream offshore. As all estuary sailors know, tacking along the shore will be faster than standing out into the stronger tide. Just how soon to tack back into the shore depends on the relative stream speeds, the speed of the boat, and just how much ground we lose with each tack. A Laser sailing in 4 knots will gain by tacking more frequently and further inshore; a 49'er in 20 knots will need to see a tidal advantage of several boats' lengths to make up for the distance lost in each tack (fig 1.8).

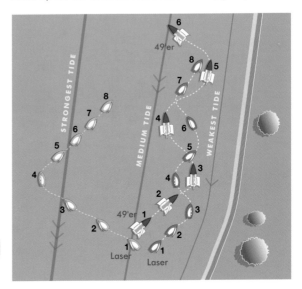

Fig 1.8 *Less stream inshore. The smaller boats can take more advantage than less manoeuvrable ones.*

If a leeward mark is on one side of a channel, and the windward on the other, we have to cross the main stream. If the side of least stream significantly changes from one section of the beat to another, again a cross to the other side may give an advantage. In both cases we choose the crossing point which gives the least adverse effect. If the stream is strengthening, it makes sense to get across early.

If it's weakening, we might leave the cross as late as possible. If there is a bay or a point which offers some short term eddy of protection from the strongest stream, we'd use this to launch the crossing.

If direction as well as strength varies over the course, by studying the information available, strategic planning can be done in advance. It's a complicated game, and very difficult to get dead right, but as always a considered plan which can be adapted, and learned from, is better than none at all.

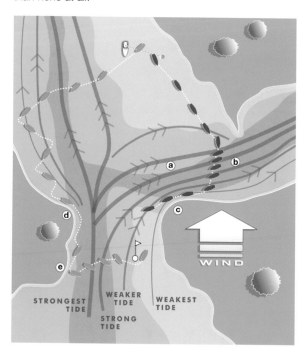

Fig 1.9 *A classic light wind beat in Chichester Harbour*

Here is a real example of a classic conflict (fig 1.9). Beating in very light wind in Chichester Harbour, Mauve opts to cross the strong stream in the main east channel (a) early, making for the weaker tide around the point (c). But progress is really slow: every time he tacks onto starboard (b) he gets pushed backwards up the east channel. Orange sees that the north channel is half the width of the eastern one: though stream strength is the same he is happy to crab across with a resultant perpendicular to the stream, taking him quickly into the slacker stream on the west bank. It gets better: once he gets to the point (d) there is an eddy, which helps him all the way to his extended layline at point (e). Once he has put enough "in

the bank", he sets off for the windward mark: though he is crossing the strongest stream in the harbour, he does not have to sail against it, merely crab back across to the mark leaving Mauve still struggling to make westward progress.

In 5 knots more wind, Mauve would have won the beat: he'd get all the way across the east stream on starboard tack and sail around (c) in the weaker stream on port tack.

How can we be sure to make the right decision, every time?

"The easy answer is: - we can't. But by collecting and checking the tidal information, and forming a logical plan, we'll improve the percentages, and gain more background to make the right call next time.

"A bit of moving water causes more debate than any other natural effect on sailboat racing. It's very easy to get confused by maths, vectors, and complicated explanations for simple effects.

"But theories don't win sailboat races: 'learning from what works', and 'sailing in the wind you feel' usually does. It's too easy to get so focused on tidal effects that we sail into a big hole of no wind, or miss the race winning wind shift. And I'd definitely recommend that the 'lee bowing the tide' argument is best saved for long winter evenings in the sailing club bar."

COACH TOP TIP

"In uniform conditions, plan for course skew and avoid the laylines (see 'course skew' page 21). In non uniform conditions, use stream effects to minimise adverse and maximise helpful current."

Waves, chop and swell

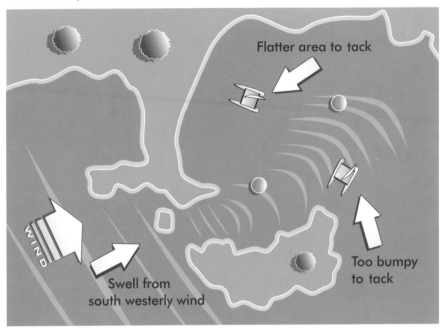

Fig 1.10 Winning strategy: tack in the smooth water!

 "At one Olympic classes regatta in Hyeres (fig 1.10), the Tornados found that the waves funnelling between the island and the mainland made it almost impossible to tack from port onto starboard. There was no problem tacking in the smoother water behind the island. Wind strength, wind shifts and tide became a secondary consideration: the only safe way up the beat was right and into the smoother water!"

A frequent issue along the seaside resorts of Britain's east and south coasts is the backwash caused by waves bouncing off a hard breakwater: up to 200m from the shoreline the waves are big, irregular, and disturbed - real boatspeed sapping conditions. These wave effects have to be factored into the race strategy: there is no point chasing increased pressure or a wind bend into the shoreline if we sail 2 knots slower as a result of the wave conditions.

 "I've also sailed light wind races in a left over swell from previous days' storms. On the offshore side of the course, we were actually surfing upwind, down the back face of the waves. On the inshore side, the waves were not big enough, and there was no significant natural asset to offset the offshore advantage."

These examples highlight that the significance of water conditions is extremely class dependent: it is difficult to imagine a large keelboat surfing upwind, but very easy to see just how much a serious chop could slow an International 2.4 m (photo page 21).

A serious chop would be very significant to a 2.4m.

Course features

Apart from moving air and water, there is a man-made set of variables which affect race strategy.

Course skew

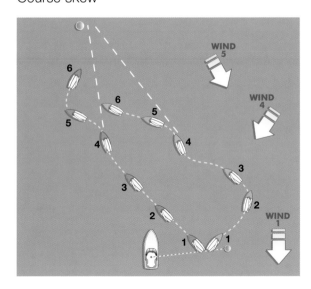

We've seen how the stream can turn a square beat into a one sided one. A skewed beat can also be the result of a badly laid course, or a permanent shift. Orange and Pink start together (fig 1.11), with Pink sailing the short leg first. His first problem is that he has to judge the layline while a long distance away: he is far more likely to overstand and sail extra distance than Orange, who sails the long leg first. The situation gets worse if there is a shift: a starboard lift (4) will mean Orange lays the mark, Pink will trail to the mark having sailed unnecessary extra distance. And if there is a starboard header (5), neither boat lays the mark, but Orange simply tacks and smugly crosses ahead of Pink on a satisfying port lift. Once on the layline any windshift means that Pink sails extra distance, while Orange can use the shift to gain ground.

Fig 1.11 *Pink's "short leg first" strategy is a risky one*

Wind across tide often leads to a skewed course. All 3 boats took the short leg first and overstood the windward mark.

 "'Bow forward on the longest tack' is a good maxim when there is no evidence of another natural asset. At least we are getting closer to the mark while we look around to see what else is going on!"

COACH TOP TIP

"The winning strategy for a skewed course is: sail the longest leg first!"

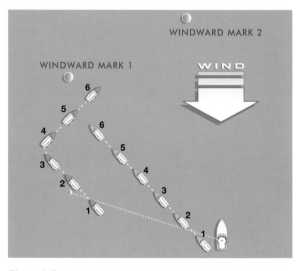

Fig 1.12 For either windward mark position, the pin is further upwind than the committee boat, giving Orange the advantage

Start line bias

Rarely is the start line set perfectly square to the wind: either one end or the other is closer to the wind. So long as boats have to sail on both tacks to reach the windward mark, the mark's position is irrelevant: in the absence of any other natural asset the boat which starts furthest upwind will be ahead when they cross (fig 1.12).

Though we usually measure and discuss line bias in terms of degrees, in order to think about strategic priorities it's helpful to translate this into boat lengths potential advantage. The longer the line (or more specifically, the further boats are spread along the line), the bigger the potential gain. Note that a direct gain of 1.4 boat lengths directly upwind equates to 2 boats' lengths of actual sailing (i.e. the actual sailing lead) if the tacking angle is around 90 degrees (fig 1.13).

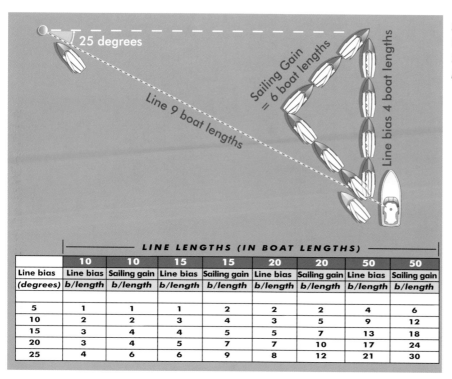

Fig 1.13 Potential gain, to the nearest boat length, for varying line length and bias angle

LINE LENGTHS (IN BOAT LENGTHS)								
	10	**10**	**15**	**15**	**20**	**20**	**50**	**50**
Line bias (degrees)	**Line bias b/length**	**Sailing gain b/length**	**Line bias b/length**	**Sailing gain b/length**	**Line bias b/length**	**Sailing gain b/length**	**Line bias b/length**	**Sailing gain b/length**
5	1	1	1	2	2	2	4	6
10	2	2	3	4	3	5	9	12
15	3	4	4	5	5	7	13	18
20	3	4	5	7	7	10	17	24
25	4	6	6	9	8	12	21	30

Fig 1.13 demonstrates that a short line with port end bias of 5 or 10 degrees gives a port end start a gain of only a boat length or so over a boat starting at the starboard end. That's less than the distance lost in a tack! If there are other features favouring the right, the boat starting next to the committee boat will control the beat. If there are no other natural assets, the boat starting at the port end will have to duck the committee boat starter when the boats cross. With 15 degrees of port bias, a start 10 boat lengths nearer the port end than another boat, making an equally good start, will give 4 sailing boat lengths advantage: enough to tack and cross in most conditions. A championship start line 40 boat lengths long would make the 14 sailing boat lengths advantage over a committee boat end starter difficult to ignore, however compelling any other natural asset may be.

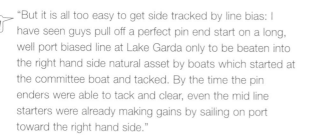

"But it is all too easy to get side tracked by line bias: I have seen guys pull off a perfect pin end start on a long, well port biased line at Lake Garda only to be beaten into the right hand side natural asset by boats which started at the committee boat and tacked. By the time the pin enders were able to tack and clear, even the mid line starters were already making gains by sailing on port toward the right hand side."

COACH TOP TIP

"The winning strategy for a biased line is: 'on a beat, start at the end of the line nearest the wind, so long as the overall beat strategy is not compromised.'"

Downwind natural assets

So far, we have looked at the impact of a variety of natural assets on upwind strategy. Of course, many of the features described also affect downwind strategy, though the priorities and details may be subtly different. We'll look at these additional variables in part 3, as we discuss each specific leg of the course.

Recommended reading list

RYA Weather Handbook   by Chris Tibbs
Wind Strategy   by David Houghton
    & Fiona Campbell
Tides and Currents   by David Arnold

Available from the RYA Webshop www.rya.org.uk

Part 1: Setting the scene
CHAPTER 2

The state of the regatta: objectives, risks and rewards

Having a clear objective simplifies decision making around the course. These objectives may change as the regatta progresses. This chapter discusses the ways in which the state of the regatta might change the strategies and tactics we choose.

 "What are we here for? Though some don't even like to admit it to themselves, sailors at every level of sailing leave home with some sort of goal or objective, however unstructured. Here are a few of my favourites:"

- *"I just want to win a race."*
- *"We are here to win the series."*
- *"A consistent regatta, no risky starts, all top ten results."*
- *"A medal"*
- *"We need a top six finish in this race to win the championship."*
- *"First junior."*
- *"I want to improve my starting."*
- *"I want to beat Ryan."*
- *"I want to avoid mowing the lawn, and finish in time for supper."*
- *"Have a nice time on the water with my mates."*
- *"We'd like to identify key weaknesses to work on before next season."*

Professional coaches and sailors use a scientific and structured approach to forming objectives and goal setting. They may break down a long term objective into shorter term goals, and simple "process goals". Process goals are small achievable stepping stones which provide the focus and pathway to achieve the greater objective: equivalent to those "bite sized chunks" which all successful "elephant eaters" preach about in business. The general message is: "identify and focus on the immediate job in hand, not the result of the race or series": if we can successfully achieve the process goals, the end results will look after themselves.

But the overall objective does have a part to play in creating a successful strategy.

"We have won an international keelboat regatta against 80 competitors with a day to spare without winning a single race. But we have also lost a dinghy championship after counting race wins and discarding a 6th place from our final score! In the first example, there was no clear pecking order and it was clear that a conservative series with no OCSs and all results in the top 10 would seal the regatta. Our objective was to win; the strategy was to do this through consistent accumulation. In the second, this extreme conservatism was not enough: we couldn't rely on the rest of the fleet to keep our main competitor back. If we had really wanted to win this series we should have had more conviction in our race strategy and starting tactics, pushing harder and being prepared to take slightly more risk to achieve the one extra race win we needed to take the series."

Our overall race or series objective can affect the strategies and tactics we choose. There are many other variables which can be stirred into the pot: let's look at some of them:

How many races?
However scientific we attempt to be, the variables affecting race strategies are never completely predictable. We can experience unexpected windshifts, pressure variations, changes in the weather pattern, or tidal anomalies. If the objective is to finish at the top after a long series, we'd expect the anomalies to average themselves out.

The more times we throw a dice, the more the average score will approach 3.5! Ryan's ultra conservative accumulative approach might be ideal for a long drawn out series.

But in a single race, especially a short one, we can't rely on averages to even things out. Roll a dice once and it is just as likely to come up with a 6 or a 1! If our sole objective is to win the race, we may have to be prepared to trust strategic predictions, push for the best start, and risk a bigger loss if we are wrong.

How many discards?
By the same logic, a no discard series would suggest the conservative series approach, while a two discard series might reward some calculated risk taking.

What has happened so far?
"With one race to go, my team is two points behind the world championship leaders. The start has been postponed for an hour, due to light winds. The strategy is clear: 'start in a space, with pace, sail to our plan, and leave the others to hold each other up'. The championships are won within the first minute of the race: while all the other contenders are fighting for the bias and slowing each other down, our team executes their plan perfectly and sails away. All they have to do to take the championship is to finish inside the time limit."

Results in the series so far can certainly change our objective, and will definitely affect the strategy.

As a series progresses the objective may change: we may be capable of a better or worse result. Once the overall objective is set, most sailors find it easier to focus on some achievable intermediate goals, for example a top 5 result in every race to guarantee qualification for the gold fleet.

As any series approaches its climax, it becomes clearer what is achievable, and what is necessary to hit the objective: by the last race the objective can be simply to beat a particular competitor, or "don't be OCS and finish in the top 10".

Size and depth of fleet

Assuming reasonably even boat speed, it's generally easier to be consistent in a small fleet than a large one. Starting consistently well is easier in a small fleet, and the errors are less punishing. Make a mistake in a large fleet, and it is difficult to follow the fastest strategy without compromising clear wind. In a small fleet a small hitch onto the other tack and back will usually achieve clear wind and freedom.

If boat speed varies, the fastest boats will usually find their way to the front of a small fleet however bad their start. Dirty wind and the sheer physical presence of a hundred other boats on the course will make an easy recovery less certain in a larger fleet. To win a small fleet series we are very likely to need to win some races, and to do this we may need to make the best start, execute the best strategy, and be prepared to get close to the edges of the course, or at least further from the rhumb line than our serious competitors. To win a large fleet series we may only need to beat most of the boats, most of the time; the safest way to do this is to keep well inside the laylines!

In a small fleet there is rarely a compromise between taking advantage of the bias on the line, and getting onto the right tack for the beating strategy: both are often possible. In a larger fleet, the rewards often come from compromising start line bias advantage in favour of freedom to follow the strategy: there is no point "winning the pin" if we are then forced out to the wrong side of the course.

Similarly our race objectives - and strategy - for a series where we have only one serious competitor would be necessarily different from one with a good depth of competition. A row of second places may win the second event, but certainly not the first!

Course style

A short course, short legs, and one lap put the emphasis on gaining an early advantage, particularly off the start line. Multiple laps might give an opportunity to play safe, and grind a route through the fleet. However a black flag start might suggest two opposing starting strategies. If we are sure the black flag will intimidate the fleet into sagging from the line, a mid line start on a good transit could win the day. If another recall is likely, a prudent starter will ensure he is "covered" from either end of the line.

Our sailing style

Some sailors are more comfortable taking few risks, keeping away from the edges, playing safe on the start line, conserving small gains, while others are more "gung ho": they want the best start, really go for the favoured side, and concentrate on extending a lead rather than defending. Both styles win races and series. We may all strive to develop and adapt our sailing styles, but there is no point attempting to win our major regatta of the year by adopting a strategy which requires us to sail completely outside our current "safety zone".

The assumption made throughout this book is that our objective is to win the race. If our objectives are different, the principles remain the same, but priorities may need to be adjusted.

"Each race and regatta presents a new permutation of variables. When building a strategy, take some time to think about the level of risk you are prepared (or may be required) to take to achieve your objective, and match this to your preferred sailing style".

Part 2: Before the start
INTRODUCTION

Pre-start objectives

At many regattas a significant part of the winning process is achieved before the start gun, or even before we arrive at the venue. This part of the book discusses various ways to collect and sort the information which will refine our decision making around the race track.

The "pre-start" period starts on the day that we decide to do the regatta, and continues through to the point we've made all our race decisions, on the water, some time after the preparatory signal, and are committed to a plan of campaign.

Tactical objectives for the pre-start period include:

Before race day:
• Learn as much as possible about the venue's characteristics, the likely natural assets, what has worked in the past and what has not.

• Understand the sailing instructions: specifically starting, course, and finishing.

Before going afloat:
• Research weather and tidal forecasts, and use this information to get a picture of what may happen during the day, and how it might affect race strategies.

• Prepare boat, mind, and body for the conditions.

Before the start:
• Check theory against reality: tidal flow and wind patterns.

• Course and start line layout

• Sorting strategic priorities

• Strategy for the race, the first beat, and the start

• Preparation for the start: laylines, transits.

27

In this section:

When sailing at a new venue (or in a different weather pattern) it is often difficult to determine just which are going to be the most important "natural assets": those external factors which are really going to make a difference to a specific race. "Sorting the priorities" outlines one technique for doing just that.

The compass is probably the most valuable tool for recognising wind patterns, vital information in forming race strategy. We'll look at ways to do this, as well as other uses for the compass both before and during the race.

For many competitors the "pre-start" is frequently under-utilised as a water resource. Few other sports give competitors the opportunity to tune and practise at will on the actual race course, just before the actual start. We'll look at putting together a routine which will help make the most of this opportunity.

Sorting the priorities

Part 1 of this book outlined the most common environmental effects which affect our overall plan, and suggested a winning strategy for each. This chapter suggests some processes which can help us to focus on the strategic assets which will make the difference between winning and losing.

How can we decide which will be the favoured side if there is more wind on the left, but less tide on the right? What if the line has a 20 degree port bias, but there is a wind bend favouring the right hand side of the course? And if there is nothing obvious, what is the strategy then?

If we race at a venue frequently enough, the pattern often becomes clear. There is then little debate about the strategy: the winner will be the competitor who most successfully executes it. This chapter aims to provide some techniques for sorting the priorities when the strategy is not so clear cut.

"Smart sailors don't worry about the little things until they have sorted the big ones. They pick out the most significant influences, decide what's going to make the real difference, and plan their race around them. On a light wind day if there is heaps more wind on one side of the course, why worry about the windshifts? Two knots wind will make far more difference! If the course is so biased you can almost lay the mark on port tack, sailing extra distance to make a small tidal gain will rarely pay. With a heavily skewed beat and a port end biased line, the first person to tack onto port will probably win the leg, irrespective of where they started on the line."

Once we are on the race course, we can check out our off the water assumptions: by visual observation, sailing the course, using the compass, and tuning against other boats. If we can eliminate some of the distractions early we'll have more time to focus on the important things on the water.

Building a mental background of scenarios and likely priorities is a lifetime's accumulatory process which is never complete: either for coaches or sailors.

STRENGTH	OSCILLATION	WIND BEND	PERSISTENT	TIDE	WAVES	LINE BIAS	COURSE BIAS

Venue

	STRENGTH	OSCILLATION	WIND BEND	PERSISTENT	TIDE	WAVES	LINE BIAS	COURSE BIAS
River	☺				☺			☺

Obviously current may be significant. Look for trees and obstructions causing wind shadows, and beware skewed beats.

Small lake	☺	☺						☺

Land based obstructions cause wind shadows and irregular shifts. Lake size may compromise course symmetry.

Large lake		☺	☺					

We are hopefully sailing far enough from the edges to avoid wind shadows! But big lakes are usually surrounded by hills: look for wind bends.

Estuary	☺				☺			☺

Similar to river conditions, tidal situation could be complicated: need a tidal atlas! Estuary may be wide enough to experience significant convergence/divergence.

Coastal

Each coastal venue has its environmental signature. But oscillating shifts are always present!

High headlands

Look for a wind bend, acceleration around the head, and a shadow behind. Could be significant in any of the above venues. (see photo 1.2) page 15.

Conditions

	STRENGTH	OSCILLATION	WIND BEND	PERSISTENT	TIDE	WAVES	LINE BIAS	COURSE BIAS
Light winds, underpowered	☺				☺			

In light/underpowered conditions, factors affecting speed over the ground are more significant than direction. Look for tide variations and areas of higher/lower pressure on different parts of the course.

Max power	☹							

An extra 2 knots breeze makes relatively small difference to vmg: factors affecting direction (windshifts) become more important.

Overpowered	☹	☺				☺		

Ensure oscillations are more significant than distance lost through tacking. Are there any areas of flatter water?

Offshore wind	☺	☺	☺					

Large less predictable shifts and light patches caused by inland obstructions.

Along shore wind	☺				☺			

Classic convergent/divergent conditions. Expect more wind on the left (N. Hemisphere). Tide may be significant as flowing upwind/downwind, and shallower water inshore.

Fig 3.1

The table (fig 3.1) lists a range of venue types, and weather conditions, along with the factors most likely to influence strategy for each one. Some venues/conditions include several categories, and there are plenty more which could be added to the list.

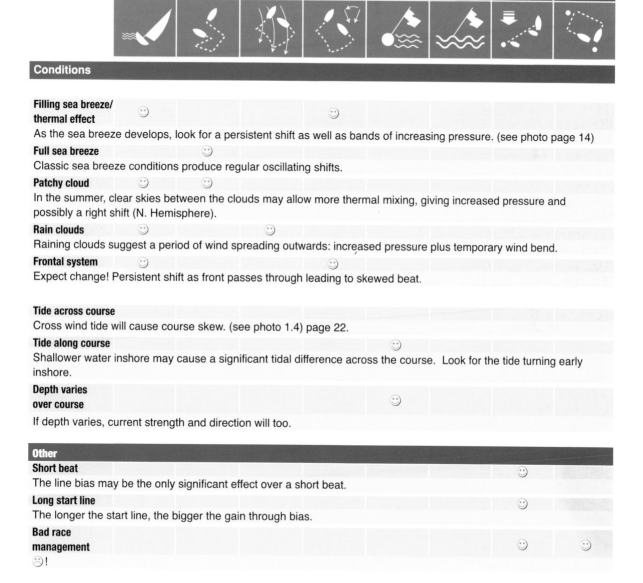

	STRENGTH	OSCILLATION	WIND BEND	PERSISTENT	TIDE	WAVES	LINE BIAS	COURSE BIAS
Conditions								
Filling sea breeze/ thermal effect	☺			☺				
As the sea breeze develops, look for a persistent shift as well as bands of increasing pressure. (see photo page 14)								
Full sea breeze		☺						
Classic sea breeze conditions produce regular oscillating shifts.								
Patchy cloud	☺	☺						
In the summer, clear skies between the clouds may allow more thermal mixing, giving increased pressure and possibly a right shift (N. Hemisphere).								
Rain clouds	☺		☺					
Raining clouds suggest a period of wind spreading outwards: increased pressure plus temporary wind bend.								
Frontal system	☺			☺				
Expect change! Persistent shift as front passes through leading to skewed beat.								
Tide across course								
Cross wind tide will cause course skew. (see photo 1.4) page 22.								
Tide along course					☺			
Shallower water inshore may cause a significant tidal difference across the course. Look for the tide turning early inshore.								
Depth varies over course					☺			
If depth varies, current strength and direction will too.								
Other								
Short beat							☺	
The line bias may be the only significant effect over a short beat.								
Long start line							☺	
The longer the start line, the bigger the gain through bias.								
Bad race management ☹!							☺	☺

Fig 3.1 *The venue type and meteorological conditions give a good indication of the likely relevant natural assets.*

For those who prefer numbers, table 3.2 uses a model which estimates the order of gains available from some major effects: calculating the strategic gain or loss in boat lengths. The model is based on a short beat: just 500m - under 5 minutes in most conditions. This enables a rough comparison between environmental factors, helping to define the priorities. Though the actual numbers are boat and specific condition dependent, this model demonstrates some pretty clear rules:

- In light (around 4 knots) winds, potential gains/losses through increased/decreased pressure are enormous: more than the difference between being entirely out of phase with a 20 degree windshift oscillation or completely in phase. However in strong winds - depending on the boat's performance profile and the wave conditions - the same increase in wind strength is of no significance upwind and may even give a disadvantage.

- In shifts as small as 5 degrees, a boat in phase with the shifts gains 4 boat lengths over one tacking at random, and another 4 boat lengths over "Shocking Pink", who gets it all wrong. The difference between "Outstanding Orange" and "Shocking Pink" increases through 16 boat lengths in 10 degree shifts to 23 boat lengths in 15 degree shifts. That's a big gain or loss on a 500m beat!

- In light winds, when there is a significant current relief/advantage available, the order of the advantage approaches that of more wind. In light winds, speed over the ground is more important than direction. But unless the tidal differences are extreme, windshifts become more significant as the wind speed increases.

- On a start line with 10 degrees of port bias, we gain 5 boat lengths sailing distance over a boat 20 lengths further up the start line. But in shifty conditions this gain may not be realised if there is a boat with an equally good start closer than 10 boat lengths to windward: our start line gain over the "blocker" is less than 2 boat lengths: this may be insufficient to be able to tack and cross. A more likely scenario is that the most windward boat, who can tack at will, hooks into the big gains available (see above) while the greedy starters allow the boats to windward to dictate their tactics.

Fig 3.2 *How much is the gain?*
Building the strategy involves prioritising a number of (possibly conflicting) effects. Though we rarely have the time or resources to calculate these priorities mathematically, it is interesting to compare the impact of these effects through a range of conditions.

There are several approximations and assumptions involved in the model used here to calculate the typical gains available through variations in wind speed and direction, tide, and line bias. The actual figures will depend on the type of boat and the day's conditions: for this model we have used the performance profile for a 21 ft sportsboat which does not plane upwind. In very light winds, a wide tacking angle is needed to keep the boat moving. Boat speed increases with wind speed, and tacking angle decreases. Best upwind angle is achieved in 16 knots windspeed, and though boat speed increases slightly up to 20 knots windspeed the actual velocity made good towards the wind decreases, as the boat makes more leeway. We can see that for this boat there is no upwind benefit if the wind exceeds 20 knots. Boats which plane upwind - particularly those with responsive rigs - do not see this "tailing off" effect until higher windspeeds, but the overall pattern and scale of gains is similar for most racing boats.

Gain/loss through more or less wind, measured in boats' lengths sailing distance over a short (500m) beat

Windspeed (k) for "Mediocre Mauve"	Position when Mauve reaches windward mark	
	Boat sailing in 2k more wind	Boat sailing in 2k less wind
4	31 boat lengths ahead of Mauve	57 boat lengths behind Mauve
8	9 boat lengths ahead of Mauve	16 boat lengths behind Mauve
12	3 boat lengths ahead of Mauve	10 boat lengths behind Mauve
16	No loss/gain	3 boat lengths behind Mauve
20	No loss/gain	No loss/gain
24	1 boat length behind Mauve	No loss/gain

Gain/loss through oscillating shifts, measured in boats' lengths over a short (500m) beat
Assumed 80 degree tacking angle: Mediocre Mauve tacks at random and makes no overall gain or loss from the shifts

Wind shift (max left to max right) (degrees)	Position when Mauve reaches windward mark	
	Orange (fully in phase)	Pink (fully out of phase)
5	4 boat lengths ahead of Mauve	4 boat lengths behind Mauve
10	7 boat lengths ahead	9 boat lengths behind
15	9 boat lengths ahead	14 boat lengths behind
20	12 boat lengths ahead	20 boat lengths behind

Gain/loss through sailing half of the 500m beat in more/less current

Windspeed (k)	Gain/loss in boats' lengths		
	.25 k current difference	.5 k current difference	1 k current difference
4	5	12	34
8	3	6	15
12	3	5	11
16	2	5	10
20	2	5	10
24	2	5	11

Gain/loss from start line bias. Measured in boats' lengths actual sailing distance, assuming 80 degree tacking angle
Gain measured over a boat starting at the unfavoured end.

Line length (boats' lengths)	Line bias (degrees)			
	5	10	15	20
5	1	1	2	2
10	1	2	4	5
20	2	5	7	10
30	3	7	11	14
40	5	9	14	19

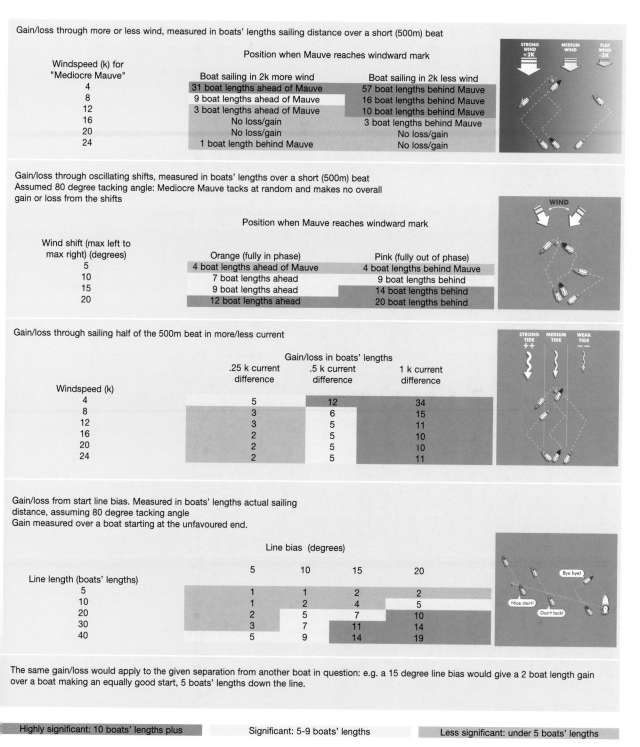

The same gain/loss would apply to the given separation from another boat in question: e.g. a 15 degree line bias would give a 2 boat length gain over a boat making an equally good start, 5 boats' lengths down the line.

Highly significant: 10 boats' lengths plus   Significant: 5-9 boats' lengths   Less significant: under 5 boats' lengths

Fig 3.2

Case Studies

In this section we will look at four very different real regattas, and use a graphical format to review and prioritise the range of strategic assets available. We've given each of the main natural assets an importance rating out of a maximum of 5.

420 Junior Europeans, 2005, Riva del Garda

The 420s sail a trapezoid course, which means that the right hand beat is in the traditional location, towards the western edge of the lake. The predominant afternoon breeze is the thermal 'Ora' blowing from the south end of the lake and funnelling into the narrower north end between cliffs to the east and even steeper and higher cliffs on the west.

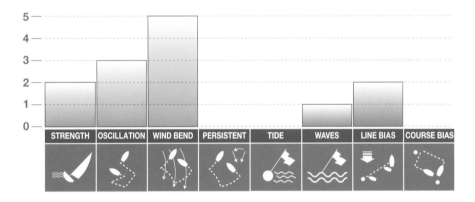

Wind strength: definitely varies over the course, with 2 knots more wind on the right hand side of the course, closer to the steep cliffs (though there are calmer patches right in the bays: (see photo page 15). However, with the average wind speed around 20 knots today we have only rated wind strength a "2", because the potential gains and losses are relatively small, except behind the headlands.

Oscillations: The wind is shifting about 5 degrees either side of its mean: enough to give local gains on groups of boats.

Wind bend: There is a big anticlockwise wind bend on the right hand side of the course. Boats which sail to the right side of the course, and tack 150m short of what appears to be the right hand layline benefit from this wind bend; getting progressively lifted until they lay the windward mark.

Persistent shift: The wind does move progressively to the right as the day progresses. However most of the movement is early when the breeze first appears, before the start, and the subsequent effect is less than 10 degrees over 4 hours.

Tide: There is a little wind blown current but it is not significant.

Waves: It's a choppy venue, but there are no significant areas of flatter water.

Line bias: The steady breeze enables the race officer to set a long line, generally about 10 degrees port bias. In theory this gives a 10 boat lengths gain from end to end, or 5 boat lengths end to middle.

Course bias: The beats are reasonably square.

Strategy: The wind bend is the overwhelming influence. The boats which take advantage of the bend the earliest, by getting onto port tack as soon as possible off the line, will make the biggest gains.

"Though there's a fair amount of port bias on the start line, the most popular way to 'hit the right' is to start at the starboard end and tack as soon as possible. But by halfway through the regatta everyone has worked this out and there is a queue by the committee boat. At the port end, a port tack start is the only way to be sure not to be forced further and further from the favoured side. But this only works for one boat: even he struggles to reach the bend before those who have tacked around the committee boat and are hooked into the bend straight away. A third solution is to use the sag in the middle of the line, reaching in on port tack across the bows of the starboard tack approachers. Good starters closer to the starboard end committee boat will tack as soon as possible: bad ones will be behind! If the start doesn't go to plan, we have identified that there are significant windshifts. Plan 'B' is to make best use of the shifts until we find a clear lane to the right, and make sure we beat the second division - who are sailing in dirty air – to the layline."

COACH!

Lark Dinghy Masters Championships in the English Midlands in Autumn

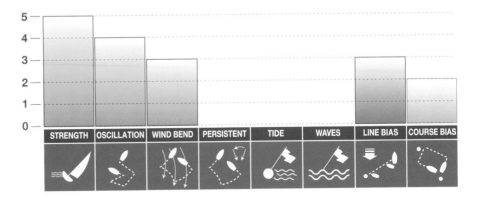

"As soon as we arrive at the lake, we can see what is going to be important. The maximum wind is about 5 knots, but there are some big flat patches. With the wind blowing down the lake, in theory we might see more breeze on the left through convergence, but there is no hard evidence of this. It's shifty (lakes usually are!) and the Larks have a reputation for pushing the start line. With more than 40 of them determined to re-live past glories,the PRO will protect himself with a hefty port bias."

Wind strength: it doesn't matter what direction we are pointing in if we are going nowhere! Wind strength rates 5.

Oscillations: The shifts are big ones, with short frequency. There are plenty of opportunities for gains and losses.

Wind bend: The wind does follow some of the contours of the lake, but these same contours are in the biggest flat spots! We rate wind bends 2, just in case the breeze fills in fully.

Persistent shift: On a small lake, the legs are so short that a steady change over the day would have no effect on one leg. In any case there is no indication of any frontal or thermal activity which would drive this.

Tide, waves: Highly unlikely!

Line bias: The legs are short, the start line is long. The loss from starting at the unfavoured end of the line is significant.

Course bias: The lake is long and thin. If the average wind direction was across the lake, a true beat would be shorter than the start line. The PRO would be forced to set a skewed beat. At the moment, course bias rates 0. But it would be significant if the wind were blowing across the lake.

"As there is no clear pattern to the wind patches, look for the next band of pressure all the time. Remember that nothing is certain on a lake: once ahead, cover the fleet!"

Strategy: Take as much advantage as possible from the line bias, but retain freedom to sail towards the most pressure. Once in the pressure, maximise the gain by tacking on the shifts. If a windshift significantly skews the beat, course bias will take over from windshifts as the secondary consideration. Get to the breeze, and sail the longest leg first.

29'er Worlds 2001, Kingston, Lake Ontario

Most races at this championship are sailed in 8 – 10 knots, underpowered conditions for the 29'er. For these boats in these conditions an extra couple of knots breeze makes a significant difference to vmg: not only do the boats start to plane upwind, the foils work more efficiently so course made good is improved as well. There is a significantly sized island to the left hand side of the race course (looking upwind). The wind over the island is 15 degrees further left than that coming down the channel, causing significant convergence on the left hand side of the course, just as the weather books predict.

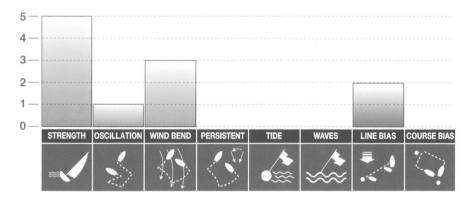

Wind strength: The convergent breeze near the island gives as much as 3 knots more breeze close to the port layline than in the middle of the course. In 8 – 10 knots that is going to be a huge natural asset.

Oscillations: There are small oscillations (5 – 10 degrees), but the wind bend and extra breeze from the land effect of the island are far more significant.

Wind bend: Even if the wind were so strong that extra wind speed gave no benefit, the wind bend gives significant advantage to the left hand side of the course.

Persistent shift: The wind has been blowing in the same direction for 3 days, with no obvious thermal effect and no forecast change.

Tide and waves: There is some current, but strength is low and seems consistent over the course. Waves are consistent over the course.

Line bias: The race officer knows his venue: to try to encourage the fleet to spread along the line he sets some 10 degrees starboard bias: in many conditions this would be an important strategic factor. However the extra breeze effect on the left far outweighs the few boat lengths gained from starting at the committee boat.

Course bias: As expected at an international regatta, the course laying is perfect!

Strategy: The biggest natural assets are on the left of the course. Start towards the port end, with a clear lane to leeward, get the bow down, and get into the escalator!

"Our few days training before the event really proved the point: the first boat to the left hand side of the course won every time! While the less prepared teams were fighting to make a gain from the starboard start line bias, ours made the best of the natural assets from the first beat of the first race, and dominated the championship from day one!"

COACH!

Fireball World Championship, Teignmouth, 2005

Unusually for a world championship, entry for this regatta is open, resulting in a record entry of 175 boats. In order to have a chance of an infringement-free start, the race officer has set an incredibly long line. With the fleet spread right along the line, and neither side of the course showing a regular gain, the leaders with one race to go are those who have been consistently in the top 10, rather than individual race winners.

The wind direction is slightly different for the last day: at last there is some land visible for a line transit. It's shifty, and puffy.
Wind strength: There are gusts coming down the course all the time. However it's difficult to incorporate this into the strategy as there are no particular areas of increased pressure. We've given strength a three: it will certainly be a factor downwind, and there may be occasional opportunities to tack late or early for a specific area of increased pressure.

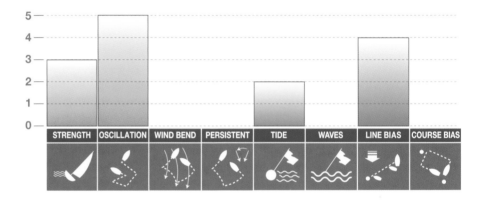

Oscillations: The wind is shifting 10-15 degrees, but the period of the shifts is very short: around 3 minutes. Shift strategy is definitely the most important factor today.

Wind bend, Persistent shift: There is no evidence or weather prediction for either of these.

Tide: There is up to 1 knot of tide, but it is fairly constant over the course, so there's no real gain opportunity. But 1 knot is enough to affect mark and start laylines.

Line bias: The line is set pretty square to the average wind direction. But the high frequency of significant shifts, combined with an exceptional line length, provide big potential gains and losses from start line bias.

Course bias: not significant.

"When the wind is right, there is a big gain from the starboard end of the line, when it's left, the port end. But these shifts are coming through very quickly: if we start by the pin and the wind lifts 30 seconds later, the whole fleet will be over us!

"The transit will give us an opportunity to make a good start nearer the middle of the line, and more chance to get in synch with the shifts as soon as possible. We'll continue to monitor the wind direction right up to our final approach. If the wind is right, we'll aim to start 1/3rd down from the starboard end, and set up to sail free and fast so we can consolidate the line bias gain as soon as possible and get to the left ready for the left shift. If it's left, we'll start 1/3rd up from the pin, and make sure our positioning allows us to tack as soon as possible, and again sail fast and free to the right ready for the next right shift.

"Strategy: Take some advantage of the line bias, without starting outside the bulk of the fleet. Get in phase with the shifts as soon as possible. Consolidate by sailing fast and free, to lead the majority of the fleet to the next shift."

"I've tried all these techniques, and still can't work out which way to go!"

The classic coach's dilemma: I have 6 sets of sailors, all wanting advice, and there is no clear pattern: what can I suggest?

- Is it possible to break the beat up into parts, with different priorities in each part? Typically, at the start of a beat towards the shore, making the most of any oscillating shifts may give immediate gains. But closer to the windward mark, we might find a clockwise wind bend (N. Hemisphere) as the wind passes the shoreline and accelerates, favouring the left hand side at the top of the beat. Beating diagonally across an estuary may suggest tidal priorities at the start of the beat, and avoiding calm patches close to the shore at the windward mark.

- Think positive: if we can't work it out, it's highly likely that the rest of the fleet can't either!

- If after exhaustive off and on the water preparation, the situation is still not clear, the strategy will have to focus on the rest of the fleet more than external effects. With no obvious natural assets on which to base our strategy, we focus on maximising any advantage available off the start line, and react to each gain opportunity as it arises - a patch of wind here, a windshift there, consolidating small gains through our positioning against the fleet. We'll look more closely at these positioning strategies in part 3.

"I encourage my sailors to treat every day as a learning day. Where are we sailing today? What type of boat? What's the history? What's the weather forecast? Is it spring or neap tides? Often this gives enough information to determine the important influences of the day. And after a day's racing or training, did we get it right? If not, what did we miss? A training/racing diary can help here, giving the opportunity to cross reference with similar conditions in the past. By using every sailing day as a learning day, my sailors are continually adding to their organic database, making next week's decisions more intuitive."

Using the race compass

A compass can't tell us which way to go up the beat, but it is one of the best aids on board for understanding and predicting prevailing wind patterns. This chapter reviews the different types of compass available, and looks at ways to interpret the data that they provide. There is also an in depth example of how the compass helped to analyse the conditions at one particular venue.

Though the appearance of the compass - and the data it provides - varies from type to type, the way in which the data can be used to improve decision-making is universal.

"Before the start, we can use the compass to help form a picture of the wind shift patterns of the day; to check for skew on the beat and the run, to predict how tight the reaches may be, and to assess line bias. Not everyone likes to record wind bearings in a table: some leave it to the coach. However, understanding the principle will help all racers to get the most from their compasses, and make best use of wind shift patterns."

First let's clarify some commonly used terms:

"Boat's heading" is simply the magnetic bearing of the direction the boat is heading at a given instant. Providing the compass is mounted square in the boat, it's the number which is read straight from a standard compass.

"Tacking angle" is the angle between port tack close hauled, and starboard tack close hauled, for a particular boat type in a particular wind condition. Most dinghies have a tacking angle of around 80 degrees, which is reasonably constant through the wind range. Most keelboats point significantly higher (tacking angle decreases) as wind speed increases.

"True wind direction" is the compass bearing from which the wind is blowing. It follows that it's possible to calculate true wind angle when sailing close hauled, by subtracting half the tacking angle if on port tack, or adding half the tacking angle if on starboard.

The boat's heading is the compass number we are sailing towards, while the wind's bearing refers to where it is coming from. So a head-to-wind boat's bearing is the same as the instantaneous wind bearing. When the wind shifts to the right (veers) the compass bearings increase (bigger numbers), and a boat on starboard tack is lifted. When the wind shifts to the left (backs), the compass bearings decrease, and a boat on starboard tack is headed, the port-tacker lifted.

"Whatever type of compass is on the boat, to really 'see' the patterns, we need to turn compass readings into something that refers directly to the direction the wind is blowing - 'true wind direction' - irrespective of which tack we are on. The system we use depends on the type of compass, but the principle remains throughout."

Types of racing compass commonly available:

Standard analogue magnetic compass:
This simply gives the magnetic bearing of the boat's heading.

	Upwind			Downwind	
	Lift	**Header**	**To get true wind angle from close hauled course**	**Lift**	**Header**
Starboard tack	Bigger numbers	Smaller numbers	Add ½ tacking angle	Bigger numbers	Smaller numbers
Port Tack	Bigger numbers	Smaller numbers	Subtract ½ tacking angle	Bigger numbers	Smaller numbers

Fig 4.1 *Standard analogue compass scale*

Fig 4.1 gives a quick guide to interpreting the numbers from a standard analogue compass.

"The great thing about a standard compass is that the numbers we use are 'real' numbers: they correlate with bearings from weather forecasts, mark bearings on committee boats, etc. The down side is that we have to use some mental arithmetic to turn the close hauled bearing into a wind bearing, to avoid ending up with two sets of numbers, one for each tack."

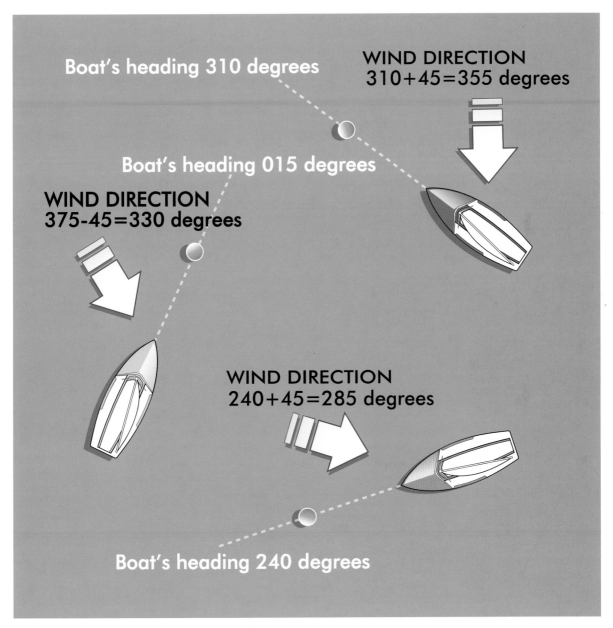

Boat's heading 310 degrees

**WIND DIRECTION
310+45=355 degrees**

Boat's heading 015 degrees

**WIND DIRECTION
375-45=330 degrees**

**WIND DIRECTION
240+45=285 degrees**

Boat's heading 240 degrees

Fig 4.2 *Converting upwind heading to wind direction*

Analogue tactical compass:

The tactical scale eliminates the need for mental arithmetic, by directly showing numbers which can be compared on each tack.

Silva tactical:

Silva's tactical scale is very popular in dinghies. The 20-segment scale, when used with the windward lubber lines, gives the same final digit on each close-hauled tack. "19" on starboard tack becomes "9" when you tack onto port. 90 degrees and 180 degrees become 5 and 10 segments respectively when checking line bias or reciprocals.

Silva	Upwind			Downwind	
	Lift	**Header**	**To get true wind "number" from close hauled course**	**Lift**	**Header**
Starboard tack	Smaller numbers	Bigger numbers	Use last digit	Smaller numbers	Bigger numbers
Port Tack	Smaller numbers	Bigger numbers	Use last digit	Bigger numbers	Smaller numbers

Fig 4.3 Silva tactical scale

"It's a great tool for giving instant feedback, but there are downsides: the scale is anticlockwise, so all standard axioms are reversed: one segment is a huge 18 degrees, detracting from precision: the tactical scale assumes that the boat's tacking angle is 80 degrees: and when you jump into a boat which uses a traditional scale compass you have to re-learn everything."

Plastimo tactical:

This has four sectored 0 to 5 scales, which give a similar effect to Silva's card, but with a more conventional clockwise scale: on starboard tack, bigger numbers indicate a lift, smaller numbers a header. (For a given wind direction, the number will be the same on each tack.) Again, using the tactical scale assumes a fixed tacking angle in all boats and conditions.

Plastimo	Upwind			Downwind	
	Lift	**Header**	**To get true wind "number" from close hauled course**	**Lift**	**Header**
Starboard tack	Bigger numbers	Smaller numbers	Use last digit	Bigger numbers	Smaller numbers
Port Tack	Smaller numbers	Bigger numbers	Use last digit	Smaller numbers	Bigger numbers

Fig 4.4 Plastimo tactical scale

"A tactical compass means there is no need for sums. This allows quicker interpretation and less chance of mistakes, however the 200 degree scale (compared with the conventional 360 degree) means that small shifts are harder to spot. The tacking angle is set at 80 degrees: about right for most dinghies but inappropriate for many keelboats, where tacking angle changes significantly with wind strength. Be careful not to get confused by Silva's anticlockwise scale!"

Digital small boat compass:

The Tacktick Micro compass, designed for dinghies, combines the benefits of conventional and tactical scales: in normal operation it gives the boat's heading, as with a standard analogue compass. In tactical mode, it shows the same number on each tack, avoiding the need for "number crunching". Since this number is the boat's heading plus or minus half tacking angle, it represents the true wind bearing, so long as the tacking angle is constant through the wind range.

Tacktick Micro	Upwind			Downwind	
	Lift	Header	To get true wind angle from close hauled course	Lift	Header
Starboard tack	Bigger numbers	Smaller numbers	Use tactical mode	Bigger numbers	Smaller numbers
Port Tack	Smaller numbers	Bigger numbers	Use tactical mode	Smaller numbers	Bigger numbers

Fig 4.5 *Tacktick Micro Compass*

The Tacktick "Master" series, industry standard for sportsboat and racing dayboat classes, has a "lifts and headers" function, which gives an instant comparison with a pre-set average or expected wind bearing. ("L 09" on either tack indicates a 9 degree lift from datum, "H 05" indicates a 5 degree header.) The Master range does not automatically correct for a tacking angle which changes during the race.

Tacktick Master	Upwind			Downwind	
	Lift	Header	To get true wind angle from close hauled course	Lift	Header
Starboard tack	Bigger numbers	Smaller numbers	Use lifts/headers function, or add tacking angle	Bigger numbers	Smaller numbers
Port Tack	Smaller numbers	Bigger numbers	Use lifts/headers function, or subtract tacking angle	Smaller numbers	Bigger numbers

Fig 4.6 *Tacktick Master series scale*

Keelboat Electronics:

Properly calibrated (and that is really important!), big boat electronics can really make use of wind bearing numbers simple. The true wind direction comes straight from the wind vane, and is corrected for the boat's velocity. Therefore, the TWD can be shown directly at all times, irrespective of the boat's speed or angle.

Keelboat	Upwind			Downwind	
	Lift	**Header**	**To get true wind angle from close hauled course**	**Lift**	**Header**
Starboard tack	Bigger numbers	Smaller numbers	Use TWA function, or add $\frac{1}{2}$ tacking angle from boat's heading (tacking angle changes with wind strength!)	Bigger numbers	Smaller numbers
Port Tack	Smaller numbers	Bigger numbers	Use TWA function, or subtract $\frac{1}{2}$ tacking angle from boat's heading (tacking angle changes with wind strength!)	Smaller numbers	Bigger numbers

Fig 4.7 Converting port and starboard readings to wind bearings, which can be directly compared from tack to tack

However, if the instruments aren't properly calibrated, there is no point using this function: it's back to mental arithmetic using boat's heading. Once into the real racing keelboat league, the electronic options are as large as the owner's pocket! Tidal offsets (speed and direction) can be displayed, and the ultimate systems show historical time vs. wind speed and direction graphs plus much more.

Hand bearing compass

The "pork pie" is a great aid, when manoeuvring the boat to check a bearing is inappropriate. We can use the pork pie to check the bearing of the start line when there is not time, or it's too crowded to sail down the line or its extensions. We can use it to locate the race marks, from a chart, from the race instructions, or from the bearing on the committee boat. If the finish line is laid during the race, it may be possible to sight its bearing as we sail past during the race, and thus determine the bias.

Tracking true wind direction (TWD)

Having gained a basic familiarity with our chosen compass, we can begin to use it to build a picture of the prevailing wind conditions.

"For as long as I can before the start (and during the race if there are enough free hands!), I note the upwind close hauled bearing in my wind log. If my compass hasn't done it for me, I convert to wind direction, or with a Silva-type tactical analogue, the equivalent number."

"To work out my tacking angle, I simply note the bearing on starboard, tack, note the bearing on port, then tack back to make sure the wind hasn't shifted. Then I subtract one from the other to get tacking angle for the current conditions.

"Rather than a table of numbers, it may help to display the readings as a simple graph. Plot the wind direction across the page, and the time down the side. Join up the dots and we suddenly get a true picture".

Torbay North Westerly

Torbay North Westerly
Tacking angle   80 degrees

Time	Course on Port	Course on Stbd	Wind direction (Course plus/minus ½ tack angle)	290	295	300	305	310	315	320	325		
9.30	355		315						X				
9.34	350		310					X					
9.38		260	300			X							
9.42		255	295		X								
9.46		260	300			X							
9.50	355		315						X				
9.54		285	325								X		
9.58		275	315						X				
10.0	350		310					X					
10.0		275	315						X				
10.1	350		310					X					
10.1		260	300			X							
10.1		275	315						X				

Fig 4.8 Ryan's wind log from the Melges 24 nationals in Torbay

Close hauled bearings have been taken every four minutes, from 9.30am (fig 4.7). (The exact timing doesn't matter, so long as readings have been taken over sufficient time to get a real picture.)

The wind bearings have been calculated from the close hauled bearings, and a sketch graph plotted to the right.

"A glance at the log tells me that this is a classic oscillating breeze. In three quarters of an hour there is no trend to the right or left, but the wind is shifting through some 30 degrees in total. These are big shifts to play with! The rough time period of the big shifts is 12 minutes - that's a fairly low frequency - providing the beat is long enough that will give an indication of how often we might expect to tack.

"There are smaller oscillations which may be useful when positioning ourselves against other boats. My strategy here is quite clear: I'll make sure I'm in phase with the shifts straight off the start line, and aim to always keep on the favoured tack. Always sailing above the mean close hauled course will mean that I sail the shortest distance up the beat. That probably means tacking from starboard to port when the compass reads below 270, and back onto starboard from port when it's above 350."

Part 2: Before the start
CHAPTER 4: Using the race compass

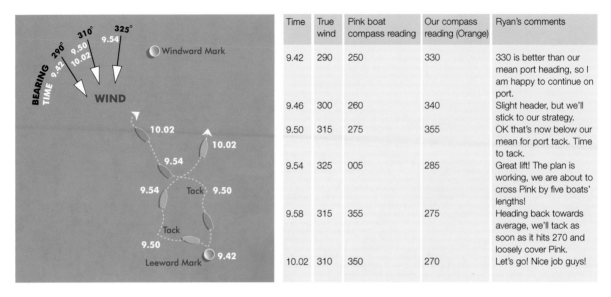

Time	True wind	Pink boat compass reading	Our compass reading (Orange)	Ryan's comments
9.42	290	250	330	330 is better than our mean port heading, so I am happy to continue on port.
9.46	300	260	340	Slight header, but we'll stick to our strategy.
9.50	315	275	355	OK that's now below our mean for port tack. Time to tack.
9.54	325	005	285	Great lift! The plan is working, we are about to cross Pink by five boats' lengths!
9.58	315	355	275	Heading back towards average, we'll tack as soon as it hits 270 and loosely cover Pink.
10.02	310	350	270	Let's go! Nice job guys!

Fig 4.9 *We've combined the wind data from Fig 4.7, with Pink and Orange's comments as they round the leeward mark together at 9.42 am.*

If Pink continues to tack completely out of phase with the shifts, and Orange continues to get it right, Orange will be at least five minutes ahead by the time they reach the windward mark. The compass has been critical in identifying an oscillating wind shift pattern, and helping Orange to make best use of the wind shifts.

Torbay Sea Breeze

"Here's a similar scenario from an afternoon at Torbay".

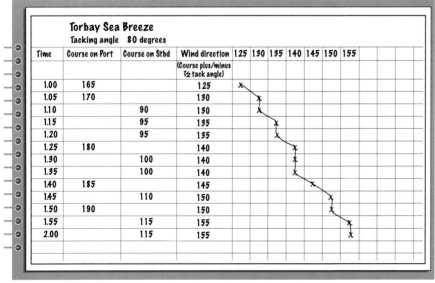

Time	Course on Port	Course on Stbd	Wind direction (Course plus/minus ½ tack angle)	125	130	135	140	145	150	155			
1.00	165		125	x									
1.05	170		130		x								
1.10		90	130		x								
1.15		95	135			x							
1.20		95	135			x							
1.25	180		140				x						
1.30		100	140				x						
1.35		100	140				x						
1.40	185		145					x					
1.45		110	150						x				
1.50	190		150						x				
1.55		115	155							x			
2.00		115	155							x			

Torbay Sea Breeze Tacking angle 80 degrees

Fig 4.10 *Ryan's pm Torbay log*

"It's a clear, sunny afternoon, and I am expecting a thermal breeze. Since 1.00 pm, the wind has been steadily moving right. I am certain that this persistent effect will continue for the duration of the race. My strategy is quite clear: head for the new wind direction (the right hand side of the course) as soon as possible. My starboard approach to the windward mark will be on a huge lift, and again, I'll have sailed the shortest route up the beat."

Time	True wind	Pink boat compass reading	Orange boat compass reading	Pink's comments
1.00	125	165	85	Excellent, we are on starboard, and its lifting! Great, its lifted another 5 degrees, keep going. We are getting near the layline, and Orange looks about to tack... hope that header comes soon! We had to tack: we got to the layline. Orange did too. No! Another header... how did Blue know that was going to happen? What did we do wrong?
1.05	130	170	90	
1.07	130	170	90	
1.08	130	90	170	
1.15	135	95	175	

***Fig 4.12** Here we have the race situation, starting at the leeward mark at around 1 o'clock. Note that Pink has done no background research, and has no wind log, so can only react to what he sees, not plan on what he thinks will happen*

"It's quite clear what happened. Pink's lack of preparation led them to assume that the wind would oscillate: not keep moving right. Orange's research and wind tracking enabled them to sail towards the new wind, taking advantage of the persistent shift."

A Mix of conditions

	Tacking angle **80 degrees**			120	125	130	135	140	145	150	155	160		
Time	Course on Port	Course on Stbd	Wind direction											
			(Course plus/minus ½ tack angle)											
1.00	185		125	x										
1.05	155		115											
1.10		90	130			x								
1.15		80	120	x										
1.20		85	125		x									
1.25	175		135				x							
1.30		105	145						x					
1.35		95	135				x							
1.40	170		130			x								
1.45		100	140					x						
1.50	190		150							x				
1.55		100	140					x						
2.00		115	155								x			

Fig 4.13 *Persistent shift superimposed over oscillations*

"It's possible that on top of a persistent effect, we will find periodic oscillations. The strategy in these mixed conditions will be to use the oscillations to work towards the favoured (in this case right hand) side of the beat.

"In this case the period of the shifts is quite long, about 10 minutes, so the length of the beat itself would be a factor in the final strategy. So long as the beat is long enough, we'd be looking at taking short starboard tack hitches, taking advantage of the oscillations to make small gains over the boats around us, while making sure that we work the right hand side of the course, defending from any boats on the right hand side of the fleet.

"And if a quick look at the compass at the end of the offwind leg shows that the wind has continued to move right for the next beat, and the race officer has not moved the windward mark, I may well be looking for an early tack: there will be no point sailing extra distance on port tack if that means overstanding the next windward mark!"

Treating an oscillating shift as persistent

If the period of the oscillating shifts is greater than the time taken to sail the beat, the effect and strategy would be as for a persistent shift. In fig 4.9 (page 48), if the beat had started at 9.30 and finished at 9.40, the best strategy would have been to head to the left of the course, as the right hand shift would not have arrived until the second leg! (See Kiel case study, page 56)

Wind bends

Sometimes the situation is confused by a wind bend: the wind blowing in a different direction in different parts of the course, rather than over a period of time. Generally the geography of a venue indicates whether this is likely, most often in an offshore breeze when the wind veers as it meets the water, or around a headland to one side of the course. As oscillating shifts are frequently superimposed over a wind bend effect, it is difficult to spot a bend by sailing upwind and logging a close hauled course. The oscillations are likely to confuse the picture. It's therefore easiest to spot a bend when going downwind, en route to the start.

"A practice run is always a part of my pre-race preparation. When sailing away from the *wind, shift frequency is much reduced: we sail away from each shift not towards it. Running under kite at the racing downwind angle, I watch my compass bearing as I sail down a practice run, to see whether any pre-race expectations on wind bends are backed up. If I spot a significant wind bend, unless the effect is extreme, I will usually treat the beat exactly as per a mix of conditions. I'd use the oscillations to work towards the inside of the wind bend."*

Sailing down the run to check for the wind bend

Beware the "Velocity header"
Many keelboats' tacking angles change significantly with wind speed.

 "In this case, think twice before tacking immediately when a lull appears to be accompanied by a significant header. You could find yourself sailing back where you have just come from! Unless your boat has a full set of calibrated instrumentation giving true wind direction corrected from the masthead vane, the only way to see through this effect is by having an accurate target speed table (fig 4.14) and a good feel which can only come from time on the water.

"Conversely, be aware a gust may feel like a lift, for the same reason."

Windspeed knots		6	10	14	18	22	26
Upwind speed knots		4.5	5.6	5.8	6	6	6
Tacking angle	t	85	74	72	72	75	80
Downwind speed knots		5	7	8	8	12	14
Gybe angle	⌐⌐	38	25	20	20	32	25

Fig 4.14 *target speed table*

Is the beat skewed?
In an extreme example, we can lay the windward mark on port tack. Now there is no point winning the pin end of the line, and waiting until the wind heads to tack and sail towards the mark. The boats which tack first will get there first!

The more skewed the beat, the more risky taking the short leg first will be: once we approach the layline any advantage through a windshift will be negated when the boats to leeward are lifted up to the mark and end up sailing less distance. Some successful dinghy sailors' strategy is always "bow forward on the long tack": though simple, this plan wins them many more races than it loses them! Checking the course skew is easy with a compass: from the middle of the start line, point the boat straight at the windward mark and write down the boat's heading. If it's bigger than the TWD (page 42) the beat is skewed to starboard, if smaller it's skewed to port.

No more strategy…

As well as measurement and interpretation of wind conditions, the compass can help us to sail the course efficiently in many other ways:

Spot the start line bias: practical method

"I like to be able to re-check the bias right up to the last minute. Once I have a transit, I sail down it, reading the line bearing from the compass. (fig 4.15). I add 90 (or subtract 90 if we were sailing up the line on port!) to get a line perpendicular. Then any place, any time, I can luff to this number. If I'm between head to wind and port tack, the line is port biased, between head to wind and starboard tack, it's starboard biased. If I can't tell, it's too close to call, but if the sails are filling, it's very biased."

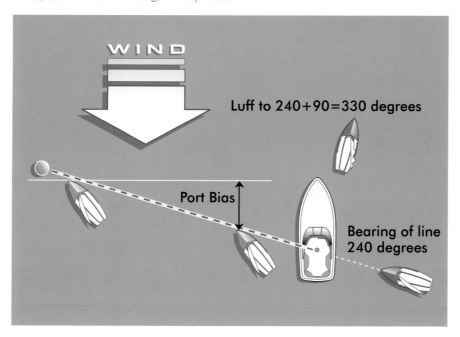

Fig 4.15 Checking start line bias

Mathematical method

If our compass gives a true wind direction TWD (page 42), or we have calculated or predicted TWD at the start time, we can determine line bias mathematically by comparing the line perpendicular to the wind ("perfect line bearing") with the actual line bearing taken by pointing down the line as in fig 4.15. This quick calculation gives the right answer even if there is a shift close to the start time.

"With each method, it's important to recheck the line angle as frequently as the transit. The anchor may drag, or the committee boat swing. It is very tempting as a race officer to pull *in a bit of extra anchor chain before the start to ensure that the Sunday roast isn't ruined by a general recall!"*

The first reach

"If the first offwind leg is a reach, I like to know just how tight it's going to be. I can then have the right spinnaker ready, and have the perfect windward mark tactics up my sleeve. For example, if it's a marginal spinnaker leg, I might sail high first and hoist to windward of the pack, hopefully driving over the opposition as they struggle to climb to the reaching mark. In a keelboat race I can usually work out the bearing of the reaching leg from a chart. In a dinghy race it might come from the sailing instructions, or there may be a chance to 'walk the course' before the start.

"On the final approach to the windward mark, I can use the wind angle calculated from our close-hauled course to work out how tight the reaching leg wil be. If the wind is right, it will be broader, and also, it will be tighter. While our competitors have to take a 'suck it and see' approach, we are fully prepared for the blast!"

The run

On the run, sailing in the headers gives the shortest distance to the mark. However, the compass is less useful, as a small increase in wind speed can make a big difference to the angle steered. This difference is generally much bigger than course changes due to wind shifts.

Additionally, because a run takes the boat away from, not into, the new wind, the time period of the oscillating shifts is greatly increased. An oscillating shift pattern upwind may disappear downwind.

"As the gusts are travelling down the course with us, rather than through us as on the beat, it's important to manage the run to stay in them as long as possible. Our first priority is to plan the gybes where we can stay in the gust, rather than merely focus on picking the shifts downwind.

"Having made that point, use the compass to choose the right gybe as follows: For wind bends, take the same side of the run as paid on the beat, i.e. we aim to sail back down the wake we made on the beat. For oscillating shifts, if headed on starboard at the windward mark, continue on the headed starboard gybe. If lifted, gybe onto port."

Back to the beat

Having learnt from the first beat, and taken some time downwind to review the decisions made, the best route up the subsequent beats should be more straightforward.

"I can use the compass to get straight back in phase with the oscillating shifts. If ahead, I will probably be looking for the first header to put a starboard hitch in to consolidate on the fleet. If behind, I am looking for the hint of a shift to tack into clear wind and make a gain. If in the pack, I must keep sight of the overall plan and not get drawn into a pointless dog fight. Keep watching for change, keep thinking. By now I should have a real feel for the wind shift patterns so far and therefore what to expect next."

The finish line

For a running or upwind finish, the line may have been laid in advance. In this case, we may be able to use the hand-bearing compass to get a bearing of the line as we pass by on a previous leg. We can compare the line bearing with the wind direction in exactly the same way as we did for the start. For a downwind finish, the favoured end is the "biased" end, i.e. the same end we would choose to start at. For an upwind finish, the favoured end is the "unbiased" end.

Informal data collection

In a dinghy, there simply may not be an opportunity to do the calculations and record the TWD numbers formally. One alternative is to periodically luff head to wind and note the boat's heading, while another solution is to note highs and lows on each tack and not attempt to convert these to a datum.

"It may be possible to understand the wind patterns with no compass at all: while coaching at Burton Week in 2004, one past National 12 champion pointed out to me that the fact that the race officer moved the windward mark to the right three times before the start (and continued to move it during the race) was a pretty good indication of a persistent right hand shift!"

Conclusion

The compass can be a terrific resource, but it does not have a brain, and can't make decisions for you. Most racers can benefit from choosing the right equipment, and developing their own individual routines based around the formal ones outlined here. As with all aspects of sailing, the biggest gains come from practice, and continual review.

When does an oscillation become a "persistent" shift?

Case Study, Kiel Week 2004, 420 class

 "After the first day's racing we have a very frustrated team. We have been starting well, sailing fast, trying to tack on the headers, but have a disappointingly inconsistent set of results to show for it.

"There just doesn't seem to be any pattern to this. First one side of the beat pays, then the other. And sometimes the leader seems to have sailed straight up the middle of the beat!"

The average wind direction remains offshore at around 270 degrees, strength seems constant across the course, and there is no tide to speak of. The big shifts (up to 20 degrees each side of the mean) must be the most significant natural asset. But how can we make the most of them?

A closer look at Ryan's wind readings (fig 4.16), taken from the RIB, start to give a clue on what is going on.

 "Though irregular, the big swinging shifts have a period of about half an hour: that's more than twice as long as a normal beat. Though there is no overall trend to one side or the other, the effect on an individual beat could easily be that of a persistent shift."

For a start at 10 o'clock, the wind direction is around 255. The beat takes about 13 minutes, during which time the wind steadily clocks right to 285.

 "That's a persistent shift. We know the winning strategy: sail into the header, toward the new wind! Next, please..."

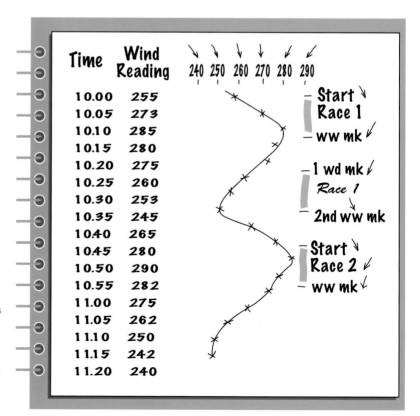

Fig 4.16 Ryan's wind log from Kiel

The second race starts at 10.42, with the wind at 270. It's 290 at 10.50, three quarters of the way up the beat, and back to 280 when the boats reach the windward mark. With hindsight, we could take the average wind direction for the beat (about 285), sail on port tack when it is left of that or starboard tack when it is to the right. (That is the winning strategy for a progressively swinging oscillation: see chapter 1 page 11)

In a real dinghy race it may not be possible to be this analytical. But once we know that the shift period is longer than the beat, and have a feel for the range of compass numbers, we can adapt a strategy to suit. Sailing on the initially lifting tack may not be the shortest way to the windward mark!

"In these conditions I'd put a lot of emphasis on taking wind readings before the start, so I am as confident as possible of the phasing of these long and progressive shifts."

"Also, remember that there is a similar effect on the last tack into the windward mark, even with short swinging shifts. If the shift period is three minutes, and the mark is two minutes away directly upwind, we may gain a boat length by sailing into the header first."

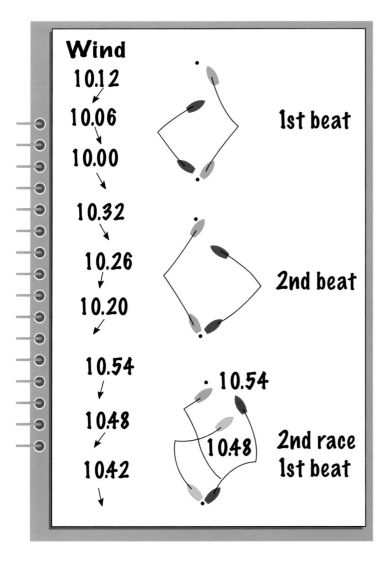

Fig 4.17 *3 beats at Kiel: 3 different strategies!*

The shifts described in the case study were uncharacteristically regular. Long period shifts are more typically irregular, with direction and period varying through each cycle. Again, the compass can alert us to these conditions, though the winning tactics will inevitably become more biased towards fleet considerations, which are discussed in (chapter 8 page 110).

The second beat of this race starts at 10.20. The wind moves from 275 at the start of the beat to 250 at the end.

"Let's go left! I'm a tactical genius!"

Part 2: Before the start
CHAPTER 5
The pre-start

This chapter looks at the two aspects of the pre-start period: that of observation and strategic planning, and preparing the specifics necessary to put the plan into action.

Pre-race observation and planning can turn occasional race winners into consistent ones: the objective of this part of the pre-start is to give ourselves the best possible chance of making the right calls: at the start, on the first beat, and for the rest of the race.

Pre-start preparation gives the tools needed to carry out these plans: where and how to start, awareness of where the laylines and start line are and preparation for dealing with the other boats.

Observation and planning

Before race day:

"If I can gain an understanding of the venue before I arrive, this will back up (or challenge) my on-the-water observation, helping me to build a clearer picture of the critical factors affecting my race strategy, and help to make the right decisions around the racecourse."

Some of this information can be gleaned from charts, tidal stream atlases, and land contour maps. An understanding of the causes of wind and tide patterns is necessary to interpret this data. See recommended reading, (page 23). Simpler sources of information come from sailors who have raced at the venue before; and from dedicated venue guides available on the internet or in magazines.

Contour maps, or road maps, give an indication of cliffs, hills, valleys and obstructions which will affect wind patterns, suggesting wind bends and compression, wind shadows, convergence or divergence.

Charts, tidal charts, and tide tables may establish whether current will be a significant natural strategic asset, where the tide is strongest and weakest, direction and strength at race time, and when the most significant changes occur.

Historical wind data from the internet may give some indication of repeating trends, as well as sea and land temperatures as indication of the likelihood of thermal effects.

Local sailors - or sailors who have raced at the venue before - may also be able to give a hint of repeating patterns. In particular, local manifestations of the sea breeze: does it fill in from one direction and steadily move right?

"I've often been recommended to 'ask a local fisherman': but my experience is that this is the best way to catch up on folklore, rather than reliable data which can be used on the race course!"

The other vital strategic information which can be digested before race day is the notice of race and sailing instructions. Reading this in advance will eliminate stress and surprises from race day itself. Of particular interest are:

- Race area: Getting this accurately defined will make any pre-regatta training more relevant.
- Course instructions: especially special finishing instructions.
- Shorten course procedures.
- Penalty and protest requirements.

If at the venue early, you can use the weather forecast each day to match visual observations (clouds, temperature) with forecast patterns, and conditions experienced on the course. If wind is mainly thermally driven, you can develop a feel for the pattern as it fills in and strengthens and there is a good chance that this will be consistent. Training on the water in the course area will give an opportunity to decide which strategic factors are weather generated, and those which are permanent local phenomena. Training on the race area also gives an opportunity to spend more time on "split tack" exercises. Use the recommended reading list (page 23) to match practical experience with theory.

Before going afloat

The most important piece of information to collect before going afloat is the weather forecast. This will help to focus on the most important natural assets of the day. (Again, the recommended reading list gives more help with how to interpret the weather forecast.)

Some examples:
- Front coming through: persistent shifts and varying pressure.
- High pressure in summer: thermal activity, likely to follow a repeatable pattern.
- Patchy clouds (especially cumulus): oscillating shifts with more wind under the clear patches.

"I look at the forecast and say…how might that affect me? Then if the forecast front does come through, or the thermal kicks in, I understand what is happening and can react appropriately."

Double checking tide times and tidal flow during the day will help establish whether tidal differences will affect strategic choices. Will it just affect tactics on the start line or round marks, or will it be irrelevant?

An honest appraisal of the results so far, the level of competition, and overall aspirations, before leaving the shore, eliminates another distraction from clear on-the-water thinking:

"If it's the first day of a long series, I may set my goal at a top five position. If it's the Britannia Cup which the owner will give anything to win just once, I may choose a different strategy."

"If you have access to a coach, make sure it's quite clear what information you'd like to have on the water: it's no good coming ashore saying: why didn't you tell me?"

On the water

"We rarely have much more than an hour in the race course area before the preparatory signal. The crews that use this time most effectively make the best decisions. Here are some of my favourite information collection methods:"

The compass: After an hour of tracking wind direction in the course area, a pattern for the prevailing wind shift condition (if there is one!) usually begins to form. Shift patterns to look for are wind bends, oscillating shifts, and persistent shifts. Chapter 4 covers this exercise in detail.

Photo 5.1 *Rabbit start from the start area*

Photo 5.2 *Tack after 3 minutes*

Photo 5.3 Big gain to the left!

Photo 5.4 What caused that then?

When they cross, the boats stop to discuss their findings. What were your compass numbers? Was any gain due to an oscillation which is time, not position, critical? Or is there a bend or a difference in wind speed which caused the gain, and will make a difference in the race?"

"If part of a squad, 3 or more pairs can begin split tacks at 3 minute intervals. This will eliminate errors due to windshifts: if a different side pays from each pair we are more likely to be dealing with an oscillating system."

What are the gusts doing? Gusts don't simply appear at the windward mark and move regularly down the course: they are frequently complex in strength, direction and position. Gusts usually appear on the water as a darker area of small wavelets. In light winds, particularly on narrow lakes or at the end of valleys, they appear as long streaks. In medium or strong winds they usually hit the water as a concentrated dark oval, which spreads out and moves in a variety of ways. Sometimes the area of dark water appears stationary or moving very slowly across the water, at other times they move down the course, often with an area of flatter water (indicating a lull) in front and behind.

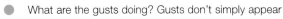

"Spending time in the course area is the best way to recognise the gust pattern. Normally, as the gust spreads out, you'll feel a lift on port if it's on your port side, on starboard if it's to starboard. If it's the sort of gust which is moving down the track, it will eventually follow the general wind direction, once this has happened there will be no lift or header when it hits. Sometimes the gusts always seem to head or lift the same tack, or always come from the same side of the

"The type of wind shift pattern is fundamental to setting my race strategy. I'm looking for data to back up the information I brought with me. Real time observations are always more valuable than forecasts, and if there is any conflict, I generally trust my on-the-water observations."

Split tacks: "Team up with a buddy, and begin with a 'rabbit start' in the start area. (One boat sets up close hauled on starboard, the other ducks his transom and sets off on port). After an agreed time period (typically 3 or 5 minutes depending on the actual leg length) both boats tack and keep racing upwind.

course: in all cases there is no substitute for sailing the course and getting a real 'feel' for the pattern."

As the race time gets closer, there may be other clues to alert you of last minute changes. Smoke from an upwind oil refinery chimney, and the patterns of other boats from the start or previous starts both provide good reliable intelligence on what may be happening next.

Check tide: this can be checked against expectations visually at an anchored mark, or more formally by dropping a weed stick or banana skin (don't forget to pick it up afterwards!) near the mark.

To get some indication of how this relates to speed in knots, use the table (fig 5.1).

Boat lengths per minute	Approx flow in knots				
	Mirror	420	49'er	Melges 24	Mumm 30
2	0.2	0.3	0.3	0.5	0.6
5	0.5	0.7	0.8	1.2	1.5
10	1.1	1.4	1.6	2.4	3.0

Fig 5.1 Converting boat lengths per minute to knots

Looking at moored boats, especially inshore, may give an indication of tide direction changes later in the race.

Look up the course, if wind is against tide, the strongest tide is likely to be indicated by the roughest water, or if wind is with tide, the smoothest water.

"We recently sailed a race in the Solent where the committee boat swung between our recalled start and the final one. The boats which didn't spot this were still struggling to fetch the start line 30 seconds after the gun!"

What is going to happen next? It's now time to put off-the-water intelligence together with pre-race observations. As well as a prediction, a feel for the confidence of this prediction will affect the race strategy.

The major questions to answer are:
- How is the wind going to shift?
- Will there be any tidal advantage in any part of the course?
- Will there be more wind in any part of the course?
- Is the beat square, or mostly one tack?

"In order to make my plan, I'm trying to use all the information I have collected so far to build a model for what is likely to happen during the race. I'll use the techniques from chapter 3 to prioritise competing factors. For example, will gaining on the shifts be more critical than avoiding adverse tide?

"If I'm really confident about the conditions, or I've decided to accept some risk to achieve a certain result, I'll use a more extreme strategy. If I'm not so certain, or want to be more conservative, I'll follow the same rules but hedge by keeping closer to the fleet or the middle of the course: using the principles outlined in chapter 8."

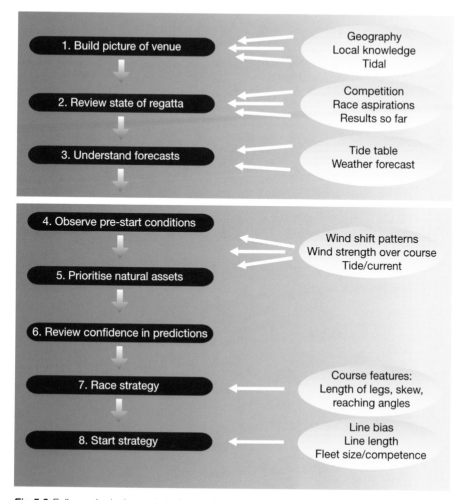

Fig 5.2 *Follow a logical pre-start plan and a winning strategy will surely follow!*

● The starting strategy

● *"We want to make the best use of start line conditions, while providing a platform for*
● *launching the race strategy. There are plenty to choose from in chapter 7.*
●
● *Don't forget that the 'best' start may prevent implementation of the race strategy:*
● *Sailing from Torbole in classic Lake Garda conditions, the race committee often sets a*
● *highly starboard biased start line. I have made the perfect committee boat start, with*
● *the whole fleet looking dead and buried behind my jib. Ten minutes later, we are all*
● *still on starboard, but all the top pin end starters have popped out in front of the jib as*
● *they hit the 'escalator' under the cliffs on the left.*
● *In Cowes week, even with a heavily port biased line, we have started at the starboard*
● *end and tacked immediately onto port into slack water, making big gains over the pin*
● *end starters who are sailing into stronger and stronger tide, prevented from following*
● *their strategy of tacking straight onto port by the boats to windward."*

The first shift

In many races, the first shift is the most important one. A good prediction of how long after (or before!) the start you need to tack onto port to get straight in phase with the shifts is as important as the start itself. In a big pro regatta, this information might come by radio, just before the preparatory signal, from a boat some way up the beat. In critical conditions (e.g. Teignmouth, (page 38); Kiel, page 56), you will probably have to make do by monitoring the compass as close to the start as possible, and by observing the fleet ahead.

The pre-start: developing a routine

With all this planning and observation to worry about before the start, it would be easy to get bogged down in theory and miss the opportunity to get in tune with wind and waves, check boat tune, and prepare for the actual starting sequence. There is more to the pre-start than being a weatherman!

"My pre-start check list (fig 5.3) helps me to make most use of the short time before the start. For an evening club race, we miss out some of the steps, but the list still does the same job, it helps us to focus on what's important, and ignore things which are out of our control."

TIMELINE	PRE-START CHECKLIST	THOUGHT PROCESS
-1 hr	Practice beat	*"I'm sailing hard up the beat in race mode, getting a feel for the wind and wave conditions, and adding to my knowledge of the wind shift patterns. Questions I am asking myself are: is the rig set right for the conditions? Do I have the right jib on? Rake? Chocks? Rig tension?"*
-50 mins	Practice run	*"Again, I'm protecting against surprises. Will we be in 'soaking" or surfing mode? Which spinnaker should we use? A couple of practice gybes get the whole crew in racing mind-set. It's also easier to spot wind channels and bends sailing back down the course, rather than beating through them."*
-45 mins	Wind patterns	*"By now I should have a reasonable feel for the wind shift patterns and be thinking about my strategy. What is the range of the windshifts? What are the high and low beating numbers on each tack?"*
-40 mins	Tide/current	*"Have I checked the current in the starting area and up the course? Does it match predictions?"*
-35 mins	Course	*"Are we 100% confident of the course? Can we spot any marks? Is the beat reasonably square? Which spinnaker will we use first, which bag should it be in, and how tight will the first reaching leg be?"*
-25 mins	Line transits	*"Hopefully by now the line is laid. Depending on the line length, I like to get a transit putting the bow around two boats' lengths behind the flag on the committee boat. The same transit will be $1\frac{1}{2}$ lengths behind $\frac{1}{4}$ way down the line, 1 length behind at mid point, and pretty useless any closer to the pin. For that reason, if possible, I look for a similar transit from the pin end as well."*

Fig 5.3 Pre-start routine

Photo 5.5 *To make this work, USA 369 needed an accurate port end layline transit*

Photo 5.6 *Instead his approach is too low, and he ends up moored to the committee boat!*

TIMELINE	PRE-START CHECKLIST	THOUGHT PROCESS	
-20 mins	Line bias	*"Once I have a transit, I use one of the techniques described in chapter 4 so that I am able to re-check the bias right up to the last minute."*	COACH!
-15 mins	Beat strategy	*"It's time to commit: how would we ideally play the beat?"*	COACH!
-15 mins	Starting objective	*"Now I can decide what my starting plan is, making the most of any line advantage without compromising my race strategy. The plan will develop around the other boats, but it's still a plan! Will the tide add to line sag, or encourage a bulge in the fleet? How fast is the slow speed drift in today's conditions? How long will it take to hit full speed?"*	COACH!
-10 mins	Start laylines	*"I try to find a transit to identify my start laylines. If my final starboard approach is above my starboard layline, I'll be in danger of being squeezed to windward of the committee boat. Ideally it's a transit which allows for cross tide and drift (see fig 6.6). If my final starboard approach is below my port end layline, I'm highly unlikely to get around the pin. Even worse, I could catch my foils in its mooring line (photos 5.5, 5.6 above).*	COACH!
-7 mins	Weed check, boat check	*"One last chance to check for weed, and get any double ended control lines down to the port side (so they are even when I pull on the vang on the start approach). Also any specifics like lining up the prop. If they are on my list, they will get done! Are we wearing the right kit? Last chance to put right or put up."*	COACH!
-5.5 mins	Ready for the warning signal	*"Boat is set, mind is set. We have done our homework, we are happy with the plan and can't wait to try it out. The warning signal comes in the next chapter!"*	COACH!

Part 3: The Race
CHAPTER 6
The start

In the pre-start routine, we built up a picture of the venue, predicted the race conditions, and formed a race strategy. We then looked more closely at the start line, checked the line bias, picked up a line transit, and made a starting plan, accepting that this may adjust depending on changing conditions and other boats.

In this chapter we'll look at using the final five minutes before the start to give us the best possible "kick start" off the start line, towards the favoured side of the beat.

 "First an example of when it all went wrong.

"It was the first race of Fireball International week, Lac de Estavayeur, Switzerland. 10 knots, and oscillating shifts were Ryan's favourite conditions. But the rest of the fleet wants to get to the first shift too: they have lined up early. Ryan is late finding his slot in the front rank, and is a little intimidated by his new (past world champion) crew: 'We have got to get up there!' They desperately reach down the line, ignoring their favourite committee boat starting spot, passing around the transoms of the waiting boats, looking for that elusive gap. 'There's one!' As they aim at the gap, the boat to windward bears off to shut the door. We have got to get over this guy.

"They desperately lunge to windward, but don't have enough pace. With fifteen seconds left, the front rankers are accelerating, but our heroes are still head to wind! As the gun goes, they are moving backwards. 'No: pull the tiller towards you!' bellows the crew.

"Then ...'Nice start, Ryan', as they are forced to peel off alone, onto port tack, while the rest of the fleet race towards the increasing pressure to the left of the course."

So what does makes a good start?

Here are some outcomes which would make most sailors pretty pleased with themselves:

- Free to follow race strategy
- Clear wind
- At the right end of the line
- Enough space to leeward to sail fast, no danger of a lee bow
- Bow right on start line at the gun
- Double speed at gun

If you can consistently achieve all of these aims, it is probably time to look for more competition! It's more likely that we have to compromise some of the wish list in order to focus on the priorities of the day.

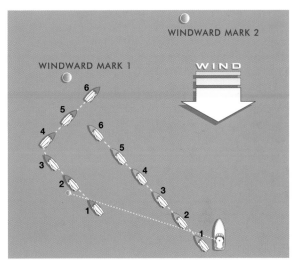

Fig 1.12 *For either windward mark position, the pin is further upwind than the committee boat, giving Orange the advantage*

"I'd just like to reinforce a couple of points.

"First, unless I can lay the windward mark, the position of the windward mark does not affect which end of the line is favoured. What's important is which end of the line is nearer the wind. If I start at the upwind end, and all else remains equal, I will be ahead of the boats who start at the other end, when we eventually cross (Fig 1.12 above).

"However, starting at the biased end may not be the only consideration. If my strategy says 'go right', a pin end start may leave me forced to do the opposite. In light winds, there is no point concentrating on positioning if other boats are able to hit the line with pace: by the time we are up to speed we won't be able to read their sail numbers! So I must have both the sailing conditions, and my overall objective in mind when planning the start."

Prioritise

Though short, the line in fig 6.1 shows about one and a half boat lengths of port bias. Since sailing boats don't sail straight up wind, this bias equates to around two and a half boat lengths of sailing distance: starting at the port end gives a two and a half boat length advantage over the starboard end. However, given the appropriate conditions, each one of the starters illustrated could be considered to have won the start:

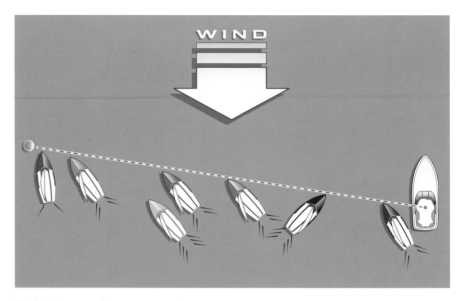

Fig 6.1 One start line, seven arguably good starts

Red: Wants to win the pin at all costs. There may be a tidal advantage to the left, or more breeze, which will create a short term advantage. This positional start at slow speed can work in lighter boats, flatter water, and full power conditions. If Red can accelerate to speed and make the lee bow stick on Orange, he will achieve his objective.

Orange: Also wants left. A two thirds speed approach is less risky in light or choppy conditions, especially if the boats are heavy and slow to accelerate. If Orange's momentum is sufficient to carry her past Red's lee bow, she will be first to the favoured side.

Yellow: Has taken an extreme "time on distance" approach. He is sailing at maximum speed, one and a half times as fast as Orange and Green. Sails are trimmed and the crew are hiking hard. In light winds racing a 40 ft keelboat, Yellow could easily be leading boat after 30 seconds. He will almost certainly lee-bow Green, and has sufficient gap to leeward to be able to sail on starboard at will.

Blue: Saw the congestion building at the port end, and believes that the wind is oscillating but in a right hand phase at present. Therefore a clear start, with freedom to tack when the next port shift comes is a higher priority than one boat length advantage through line bias. So long as there is no big left hand advantage, Blue will be able to control the leeward starters (though ahead, none will be able to tack and cross), and choose his tack onto port.

Indigo: Believes that the right hand side of the course is favoured, took a look at the fight for the pin, and realised that an early port tack from the pin end would be difficult to achieve. She bailed out in plenty of time, ducking Blue at full speed to hit the line at reaching speed going in the direction she wants. She is able to cross Violet and be first to the right.

Violet: Also believes right is right. However leads the series and saw no reason to risk a port tack start. By making a safe conservative starboard start she still has the opportunity to tack below Indigo and be first to the right, or call Indigo across and shadow the majority of the fleet with a small right hand advantage.

"We can see that good starting is not just about having a theoretical lead five seconds after the start gun. It is about focusing on the priorities which are important for the coming beat, and reacting to changing situations (other boats) to ensure that those priorities are achieved."

Fig 6.2 suggests 6 potential starting strategies, likely favourable scenarios for each, with key execution tips.

Approach	Description	Good for	Not recommended for
Port tack approach	As the body of the fleet lines up on starboard, we approach on port tack, looking for a well positioned boat with a reasonable gap to leeward. By tacking to leeward of this boat, we effectively steal his space, while using him as cover from the committee boat and defender from boats to windward.	Even biased line Plenty of spaces Specific people to beat Even beat	Very port biased line Congested fleet Light winds Right hand paying beat
The "hook"	Sailing on starboard from behind and to windward of a bunch, we take the transom of a well positioned boat who has space to leeward, then luff, killing our speed and positioning us as for port tack approach.	Starboard biased/even line Fleet lined up early	Port biased line Light winds Quickly accelerating boats Fleet lined up late
The "charge"	With 30 plus seconds to go, we use time on distance skills to find a route through the slowly moving pack: hitting the line at full speed while those around are still trying to accelerate.	Heavy, slow accelerating boats Even/starboard biased line Fleet lined up early	Port biased line Fleet lined up late Congested line
Lead in on starboard	We keep bow forward on the boats around us, luffing and slowing boats to windward, if necessary reaching over the bows of boats to windward. We accelerate first and lead the fleet over the line.	Port end start, port biased line Fleet lined up late	Fleet lined up early
Port tack start (photos 6.14-6.16)	With perfect time on distance we hit the pin on port tack and cross the fleet. Alternatively duck the good starters at the port end and cross the rest.	Port biased line with starboard favoured beat Insurance companies Light winds	Nervous skippers Starboard biased line Port favoured beat
The "slide"	We set up on starboard, high of the main pack. As the fleet drifts sideways we control our drift, and arrive at the back of the starboard committee boat with a gap to leeward and time to accelerate to speed.	Strong winds Even line	Light wind Starboard biased line

Fig 6.2 *Six starting approaches, with key points and recommended applications*

Starting tools

Having decided priorities, there are a number of skills which are required to get the boat in a position to achieve them. All are gained and improved through practice.

Where is the line?

Boats which get consistently good starts have at least one person on the boat with the skill to know just where the line is. To reinforce and learn this sixth sense, here are some techniques for spotting the line.

The transit

Though often hidden in a big fleet close to the start signal, the transit can be used to set up on a specific station say one minute before the start. It can be used in practice to sharpen other senses, and it also makes line bias quicker to check. If you are able to locate the line transit at the start gun, you can accelerate with confidence.

"I pass slowly by the committee boat, outside the start line, and when the committee boat flag lines up with the pin end, pick any conveniently sited oil refinery on the shore which is dead in line with pin and committee boat (fig 6.3). Now when I approach to the line, if the refinery is on the course side of the pin, so are we. If it's behind, so are we. To sail straight down the line, keep pin and refinery in line. To be precise, the person sighting is on the line, and any part of the boat in front is over."

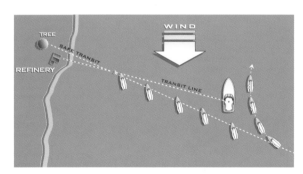
Fig 6.3 *The tree gives a safe transit, the refinery is right on the start line*

"I like to get a transit putting my bow around two boats' lengths behind the flag on the committee boat. This transit will be one and a half lengths behind, a quarter of the way down the line, one boat length behind in the middle, and pretty useless any closer to the pin. For this

reason, if possible, I look for a similar safe transit from the pin end as well."

Sighting the line

Some people are able to "see" the start line drawn on the water, from committee boat to pin. Sail slowly parallel to the line, in the starting area. Face directly upwind, and sight at committee boat and pin. Compare your feel with the transit. Any correlation? This really does only work for "some people".

The Goodison

Top Laser sailor Paul Goodison has a simple solution: "From any position along the line, I point my bow at the pin. Holding the tiller dead central. I sight down the tiller. If I'm looking in front of the committee boat, we are over the line. If I'm looking behind, we are OK."

The Charles

The late Glyn Charles, GBR Olympic sailor and Laser champion, once defended an OCS hearing using a hand bearing compass. By writing down the bearing of the line and its reciprocal (subtract 180 degrees) a sight of either end would indicate whether he was over the line, or safe.

How long to the start line?

Start with a good match racer and you may hear a persistent mumbling in your ear. Listen and you might find it useful. Good match racing requires not just accurate judgement of the line position, but a sense of how far away it is in terms of time. Learning this skill enhances time on distance starting techniques.

"Learn to judge and call how many seconds sailing you are from your chosen point on the line in your boat, in the prevailing conditions. Use this knowledge to judge when to hit full speed as the gun approaches, when to bale out because it's not going to be possible to hold back, and when to start the final approach without getting caught too far from the line through concentrating on other boats. If you are confident of your intended starting position on the line, reinforce this information with a transit say 30 seconds slow sailing from the line (but don't forget that if you half the distance to the pin, you half the sailing time from this transit to the line!"

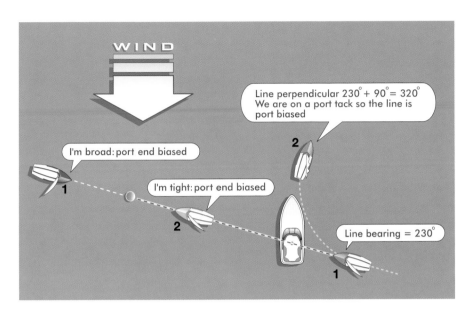

Fig 6.4 *Checking the start line bias with and without a compass*

Spotting the line bias

"I like to use my compass to re-check the bias right up to the last minute. Once I have a transit, I sail down it, reading the line bearing from the compass. I add 90 (or subtract 90 if we were sailing up the line on port!) to get a line perpendicular (fig 6.4). Then any place, any time, I can luff to this number. If I'm between head to wind and port tack, the line is port biased, if between head to wind and starboard tack, it's starboard biased. If I can't tell, it's too close to call, but if the sails are filling, it's very biased!"

It is also possible to spot the bias without a compass, by sailing up and down the transit, noting on which tack the boat sails at a broader angle to the wind. If, when sailing along the line, starboard tack is broader, the line is starboard biased. If port tack is broader, it is port biased. Another alternative is to luff head to wind on the start line, then sight down a perpendicular to the centreline, for example, the traveller. The favoured end will appear upwind of the perpendicular.

"One final point on start line bias: beware of using the flags on anchored marks or committee boats to check wind direction in tidal venues (fig 6.5 page 72). The race committee have anchored, and laid a line which is perfectly square to the wind. But the tide has shifted the effective sailing wind (fig 6.1 page 68). The tide causes the sailing wind to be shifted to the right, so the line is port biased. A line set square to the true wind will be biased towards the down tide end!"

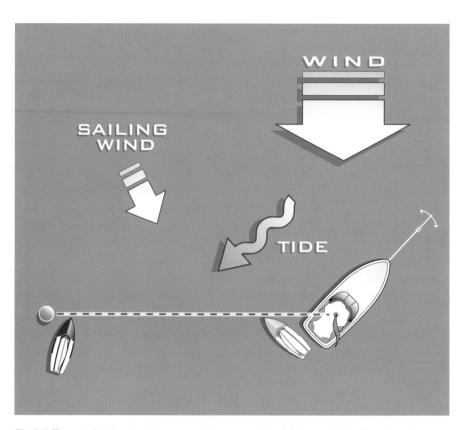

Fig 6.5 *Though the line is set square to the ground wind, it is port biased to the sailing wind*

Boat handling

Boat handling and boat awareness are the key tools required to get the boat in the right place at the right time. The only way to develop boat handling skills is to practise, through the range of sailing conditions, until the answers to these questions are instinctive:

Stopping quickly without luffing.
- Holding the boat on station or "slow forward", in a close hauled direction, with sails flapping how much leeway is made through the range of conditions?

Turning the boat without accelerating, using sails and body weight.
- What is the most effective technique to bear away fast to close a gap, without acceleration? Then luff back to preserve height.

Acceleration from slow forward mode.
- How much time is needed in the range of conditions? How much of a gap to leeward is required?

Now let's look at how Ryan puts these skills together to achieve three classic starting scenarios.

Nail the Pin

"To win the port end, I want to control the fleet. First I set up for an accurate starboard tack time on distance approach."

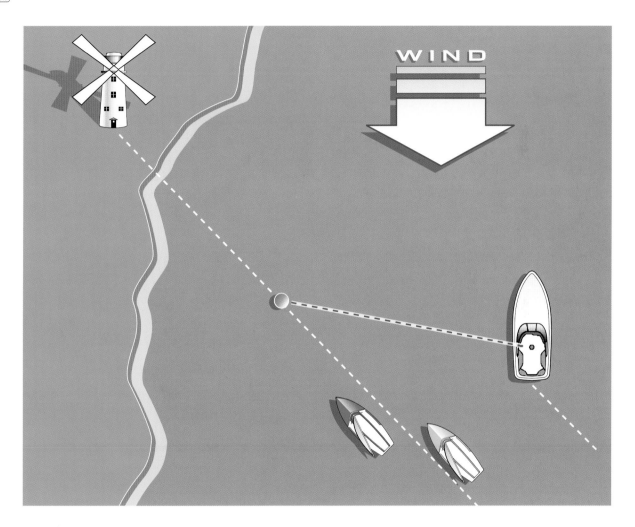

Fig 6.6 The windmill provides a transit for the pin end layline. Blue is below the layline and will not get around the pin without tacking. Yellow is perfectly placed to accelerate to the pin.

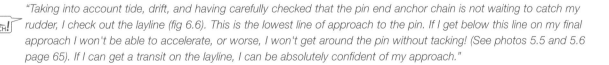

"Taking into account tide, drift, and having carefully checked that the pin end anchor chain is not waiting to catch my rudder, I check out the layline (fig 6.6). This is the lowest line of approach to the pin. If I get below this line on my final approach I won't be able to accelerate, or worse, I won't get around the pin without tacking! (See photos 5.5 and 5.6 page 65). If I can get a transit on the layline, I can be absolutely confident of my approach."

The perfect pin end start

Photo 6.1 *The two ISR boats show their intentions early on this port biased line*

Photo 6.2 *GER sails from the port end towards his chosen spot*

Photo 6.3 *GER bears off to leave room to tack close below ISR*

Photo 6.4 *NOR has a similar plan*

Photo 6.5 *GER bears off hard to defend his space*

Photo 6.6 *NOR is forced to duck then tack to windward*

Photo 6.7 *GER in control, luffs to hold the fleet up until he is ready to accelerate*

Photo 6.8 *GER bears off ready for acceleration*

Photo 6.9 *GER sails as fast as possible at the pin*

Photo 6.10 *As the gun goes, GER is the only boat at maximum speed and in clear air*

Photo 6.11 *After just 5 seconds, GER is already a boat length clear and extending*

"Don't forget, that the more the line is port end favoured, the harder it will be to reach it on starboard tack. If the wind shifts right, the starboard approach will be quicker." (fig 6.7)

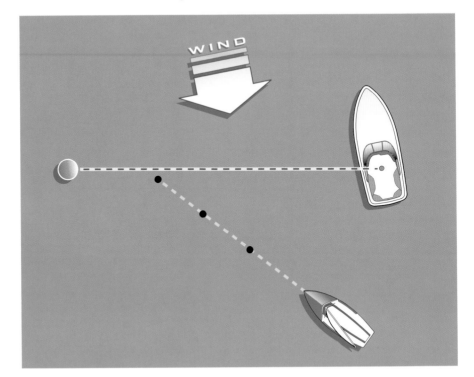

Fig 6.7 The blue boat is two boat lengths distance from the nearest part of the line in each case. But when the line is port biased, he's more than three boat lengths sailing distance away. When it's starboard biased, he's just two boat lengths sailing distance away.

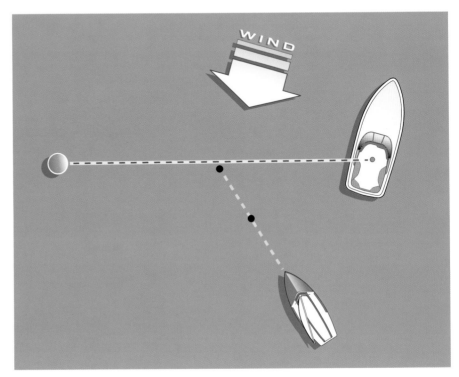

"There is a fair bit of psyche on a pin end start. If our competitors see us manoeuvring around the pin, making a practice approach, looking generally confident, they will most likely go for a less aggressive start further up the line. At around about two minutes from the gun, I'll aim to be somewhere near the pin, watching the fleet set up. The pack on starboard will be making their approach from to leeward of the committee boat. If there are any other pin end pretenders near me, I will try to sweep them up towards the pack, by tailing them on port, with my bow just off their transom. From here I can force them up towards the pack by putting my bow below their transom, and stop them tacking by sticking my nose up. Eventually they have to ask for room to tack on the pack, and I tack as close as possible under their lee bow (or the lee bow of the first starboard approacher). With a minute to go, I am aiming to be the Blue boat in fig 6.8. Now all I have to do is to hold the fleet up, maintaining the overlap to prevent them reaching below me or powering over me, until my time on distance tells me I can let them go and accelerate for the pin. I point one boat width below the buoy, wind everything on and hike to max speed, luffing to close hauled in the final seconds.

"To defend from another approaching port tacker, I bear off hard and aggressively, aiming below his bow. If he tacks, I want him to do it below the layline. If he passes to windward, great. If he manages to tack to leeward but above the layline, I have two choices. If I am sure I can make it through his dirt and there's room above the layline (fig 6.6) I scoot below his transom with speed, and luff back, to regain control. If not, I luff high using the speed I gained, and create a gap to accelerate into later. And I remember to be more aggressive next time! If my approach was well judged, he will struggle to combine acceleration, staying behind the line, and laying the pin.

"To defend from a boat reaching down on starboard tucking up under my transom, I bear away hard, making the gap to windward look really inviting. Keeping an eye on the layline, and the distance to the pin, I lead him down towards the pin, preventing him from establishing a leeward overlap. I only let him through if he is going to end up early for the start, or below the layline. In that case, I use the speed to luff and create my acceleration gap."

Cuff the committee boat

It's much more difficult to control a starboard end start, as it is not possible to herd or to predict the actions of the other boats in the same way as for the pin end approach. A good starboard start needs good boat control skills, and quick reactions to changing circumstances. The only way to get better at it is to practise!

"I identify the starboard tack layline to the committee boat. If I set up too far above this, I am in danger of being squeezed out by leeward boats. If I set up below, I can't take advantage of any spaces near the committee boat. Again, a transit, this time for the starboard tack layline to the committee boat, helps me to judge this. With two minutes to go, I like to be around 10 to 15 boat lengths from the line, somewhere just to windward of the layline, just watching how the fleet sets up. If it looks like it's going to be a nightmare, I still have time to bale out and start mid line.

"If I'm happy that the volume of traffic allows an opportunity for a committee boat start, I join the front rank of boats. If the windward boat is above the starboard layline, I'll find a gap below him, using the 'hook' (fig 6.2) page 69. If he's below, I'm happy to set up to windward. I concentrate on defending my piece of water from encroachers, while keeping an eye on time to the line. I spot bargers early, and give them a clear verbal warning. I defend from luffing boats to leeward by either keeping far enough forward that I can sail over them, or by ducking their transom with speed then returning the favour. I deter boats coming from behind from taking my gap by bearing away sharply to make it look less inviting (pushing boom out to prevent acceleration), then luffing to 'regroup'."

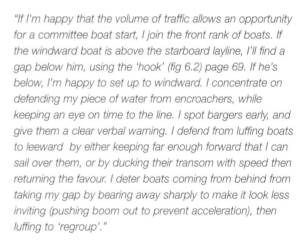

Photo: 6.12 *The boat on port has tacked to reach the gap which has appeared above the group*

"As time goes by it becomes clear if the fleet is generally going to drift away from the committee boat. If this is the case, two quick tacks will find me a space to windward (photo 6.12). With 1 minute to go, I continue to defend my part of the start line. I judge my 'trigger' (the time to sheet on) from the pack, and from my distance to the line. Unless it's very light wind I really don't like trying to find a way through parked boats using a timed run approach, so rely on my ability to defend my leeward gap. I can use this gap to accelerate better than the pack, keeping an eye on my transit or other line indicators at the same time.

"If I find that I have set up above starboard layline, I would move too far forward by just bearing away. Instead I can accelerate my drift and move in sideways: I luff above close hauled, playing the windward jibsheet to prevent an involuntary tack. I keep the tiller hard away, and in a centreboarder may lift the plate a little. Now that all foils are stalled, I drift sideways with no forward motion. When using this technique I need to leave enough room to leeward to bear away and get control before drifting too close to leeward boats!"

In the middle

"For me, 'mid line' is anywhere further than five boat lengths from an end. 'Ahead of the nearest boats' is the key objective. If I have a good line transit, and there is a clear line sag, I don't give this information away by sitting three boat lengths in front of the pack, I wait until 10 seconds to go and then surprise everyone with my confidence. I always approach a mid line start on port tack. I am looking for a bunch of friendly looking starboard tackers, preferably boats I know who aren't aggressive starters. I am looking for a gap. Not too big, or the person following me will come and ruin it. A boat length is good. I can close a boat length's gap by bearing away, to encourage predators to try somewhere else. With 1½ minutes to go I tack into my space, close under the most leeward boat. The heavier the boats are, the further back I tack. This gives me plenty of chance to match speed and prevent the windward boat ducking my transom (Fig 6.8).

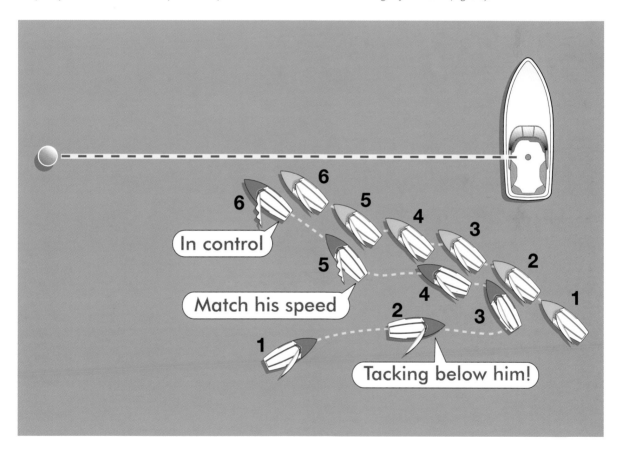

Fig: 6.8 Blue tacks behind and to leeward of yellow, then matches speed to take control

"In a bigger fleet I may have to line up earlier as the front row may fill early! I aim to keep my bow back as far as possible without the windward boat blanketing me. This way I have a couple of feet more space to accelerate into. Now I defend the space from port tackers and starboard reachers as I've already outlined. In the final thirty seconds, our eyes are out of the boat watching for anyone making the first move. Kicker, Cunningham, jib cars are all set up for maximum pointing: with a mid line start we absolutely have to be sailing fast and high with five seconds to go. I'll probably use half of my leeward gap to create speed in the last ten seconds, and save the rest for the race!"

Which rules apply?

It's important to be confident of your rule knowledge, and equally important that your competitors respect this. A clear (but polite!) hail establishing the status quo will generally establish this respect and prevent an incident. But first you have to do your homework: spend some time with your rule book and familiarise yourself with these concepts:

Keep clear: Just because there is a gap between a windward and leeward boat, it does not necessarily follow that the windward boat has kept clear.

Rule 11, 16: A boat to leeward can luff to head to wind. But each time it changes course, it must give the windward boat room to keep clear.

Rule 12: A boat clear ahead on the same tack has no obligation until the boat behind physically establishes an overlap to leeward. Shouting "up up up" when clear astern means nothing.

Rule 15: The boat establishing the overlap to leeward has to *initially* give the windward boat room to keep clear. But the windward boat must immediately react: "initially" is an instantaneous situation. Once the leeward boat has given this initial room, the windward boat must keep clear, including avoiding drifting sideways onto the leeward boat.

If the leeward overlap occurred because the windward boat bore away, and changed the angle of its transom, so long as the leeward boat did not change course, it does not have to give room.

Rule 13: Once a boat luffs past head to wind, it is tacking until it bears off to a close-hauled course. A boat that luffs past head to wind to close a windward gap, or tacks below a starboard tacker, and stays above a close-hauled course, therefore has no rights until it bears away to close-hauled.

Suggested reading: 2005-2008 RYA Racing Rules   Order Code Y R I
To order: ring 0845 345 0400 or from the RYA webshop www.rya.org.uk

The beat

Part one and two of the book reviewed the main features which contribute to the "fast and slow lanes" around the race track. But we now have to apply this intelligence in the context of a real race, with a course full of other competitors.

Chapter 6 has hopefully given us a fantastic start, with every opportunity of following our racing strategy: what next?

The first part of chapter 7 (page 83) splits the beat up into parts, and discusses the way in which our decision making priorities change as we proceed up the beat. It also discusses the options available when boats cross: "dip, tack, or call".

The second part deals with our positioning against the rest of the fleet: maximising and consolidating gains, and managing risk.

Part 3: The Race
CHAPTER 7
The beat 1: Tactical priorities

In chapter 6 we discussed how to turn pre-start plans into reality, looking at choosing a starting strategy which takes account of local factors such as start line bias, but allows quick adoption of the overall strategy for the beat. We also looked at ways to escape from a bad start.

The start gun has now fired, and Ryan is about to guide us up the first beat.

 "To focus the mind, I divide the beat up into parts. Each part has a different set of priorities. With clear priorities, the decisions I need to make as the race progresses become clearer, and more intuitive."

Phase one: clear wind

In chapter 1 (page 9) we compared gains and losses available from various natural assets, over a short (500m) beat. Using the same principle, a boat that sails the whole beat 10% slower and 3 degrees lower than our model, in 10 knots breeze, loses around 16 sailing boat lengths. That is a fairly typical performance reduction when beating two boat lengths directly downwind of a boat of the same class. That's more than we gained from most windshift models! Worse still is that two boat lengths lost in the first 10 boat lengths of the race probably contains half of the fleet. Sailing for 10 boat lengths off the line in dirty wind will let half the fleet past. Any other strategic asset will have to be pretty big to make up for that!

 "If the start was good, I should be able to move straight on to the next phase. If not, it may be clear that everything is going wrong a minute before the gun. In this case, I start wriggling straight away. I am usually looking for an early port tack escape route. I must anticipate the actions of the boats around: it's no good blindly tacking onto port only to have the boat immediately to windward do the same."

After the start, it is often possible to maintain clear wind by sailing slightly free and advancing forward of the danger zone from the boat to windward. This tactic can be used to gain time until a suitable port tack lane opens up. As boats start to tack and cross, it is possible to manipulate the situation to reserve that all important clear lane.

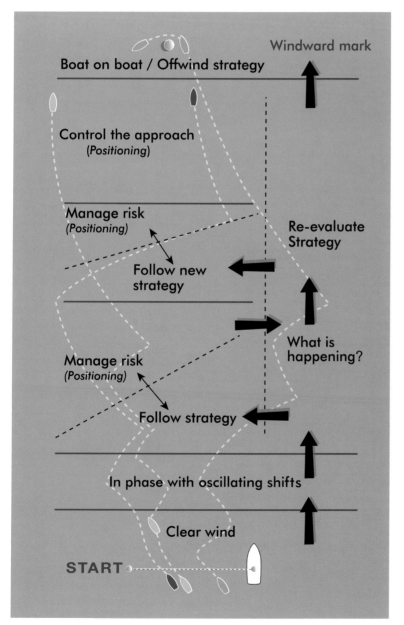

Fig: 7.1 The beat split into sectors

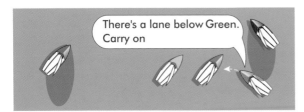

Fig: 7.2 *Grey looks for a lane on port*

Grey is starting to feel the effect of Black's wind shadow, but can't tack without receiving the same treatment from Blue or Yellow. Bearing off encourages Blue to continue on port, and moves Grey forward into a clear wind situation (fig 7.2).

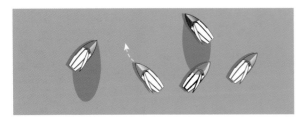

Fig: 7.3 *Grey tacks safely to leeward of Green*

Grey now chooses to tack into the port lane between Green and Yellow (fig 7.3). Grey is now free to tack at will, has a clear lane, and has positioned herself so that Black is far more likely to tack on top of Green than on Grey (fig 7.4).

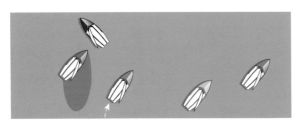

Fig: 7.4 *Grey is in clear wind, going in the right direction*

"We have all had races where we are still fighting for clear wind after 10 minutes or more. The layline is approaching; we have missed the shifts, and have failed to follow any part of our strategy. As a result most of the fleet is now ahead! We'll talk about recovery later, but if this is a repeating scenario, it is probably time to go back to starting practice, or work on upwind boat speed."

Phase two: in phase with oscillating shift

The first shift is critical: often the most important of the race. The pre-start routine has given a feel for period and size of any oscillating shifts. Getting in phase with the oscillations before the other competitors will produce an immediate gain. At this stage of the race, a gain of just a few boats' lengths gives clear wind, and freedom to follow pre-set plans.

"In oscillating conditions, my pre-start compass readings have given me a good indication of best headings for port and starboard tack. I have a feel for what the average heading is on each tack, and, once my air is clear, I make sure that I'm on the tack which takes me higher than average (that's a smaller compass number on port tack, a bigger number on starboard)."

Spotting the shifts without a compass

Fig 7.5 *Boats are even*

Noting compass numbers is the simplest way to observe windshifts. With no compass it's possible to distinguish lifts from headers by referring to the fleet. In fig 7.5 boats are equally progressed towards the wind.

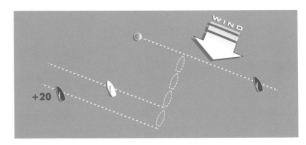

Fig 7.6 *Starboard lift*

In fig 7.6, Blue notices White and Red disappearing behind his jib: it's a lift. In fig 7.7 they are popping out in front, and Blue is starting to point towards them: it's a header. In oscillating shifts, they appear and disappear regularly, while in a wind bend or a persistent shift, they keep moving in the same direction.

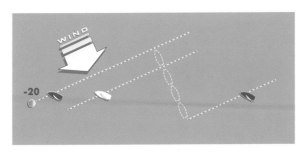

Fig 7.7 *Starboard header*

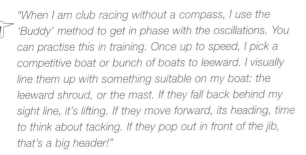

"When I am club racing without a compass, I use the 'Buddy' method to get in phase with the oscillations. You can practise this in training. Once up to speed, I pick a competitive boat or bunch of boats to leeward. I visually line them up with something suitable on my boat: the leeward shroud, or the mast. If they fall back behind my sight line, it's lifting. If they move forward, its heading, time to think about tacking. If they pop out in front of the jib, that's a big header!"

Beware the velocity header: just as when using the compass, be suspicious of a header and lull or a lift and gust, arriving together. The heading change may simply be due to the boat's characteristics changing with wind speed. (see chapter 4 page 52)

Phase three (i): follow the strategy

In parts 1 and 2 of the book we discussed the rationale behind taking the available time before the start, off and on the water, to understand prevailing conditions, and form a race strategy. This is the underlying plan on which decisions are based as the race proceeds. The strategy also gives an opportunity for learning and improvement: if it worked, we can use it again. If not, we have an opportunity to work out why not, and make it better next time!

America's Cup boats have both strategists and tacticians: though the roles are interdependent, strategy is more concerned with the "big picture". Tactics are the tools used to achieve the strategy. Tactics involve an immediate reaction to external influences: other boats, short term wind effects, mark rounding decisions, etc. Tactics are also the tools we use to manage risk.

"If I can understand the wind shift patterns, I am usually close to getting my race strategy right. But every day and every venue has its particular priorities. When racing at Cowes in spring tides, for example, making best use of the tide is usually more important than sailing to the inside of a bend around a headland."

Special conditions

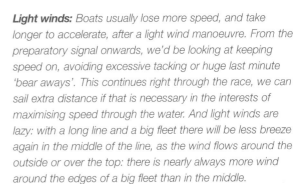

"I'd like to highlight a couple of special conditions which may affect our tactical considerations around the race course, in just the same way that strategic priorities in Chapter 3 (page 33) changed depending on conditions:

Light winds: *Boats usually lose more speed, and take longer to accelerate, after a light wind manoeuvre. From the preparatory signal onwards, we'd be looking at keeping speed on, avoiding excessive tacking or huge last minute 'bear aways'. This continues right through the race, we can sail extra distance if that is necessary in the interests of maximising speed through the water. And light winds are lazy: with a long line and a big fleet there will be less breeze again in the middle of the line, as the wind flows around the outside or over the top: there is nearly always more wind around the edges of a big fleet than in the middle.*
Small fleets: *To win races and series in small fleets usually needs more emphasis on the 'fastest course' and less on the 'risk management'. That's because the fastest boats usually make it to the front of the race in any case: a bad start or small mistake is not likely to send them chasing to the wrong side of the course in search of clear wind. If we are too conservative, we'll never get a chance to challenge the leaders.*
Big fleets: *Conversely, consistency often wins series in large, competitive fleets. Consistency usually comes from good risk management."*

Keeping clear wind

We have already talked about the importance of clear wind in the first five minutes, which is critical. Clear wind is easy when we are in the top 10% of the fleet. When in the pack, we need to keep clear wind without being forced to the lay line, or deflected from our strategy.

"Anticipation is the key. I don't wait until the shift arrives, the starboard tacker shouts, or the enemy tacks on me before looking for the escape route. I look upwind at the patterns in the fleet, spotting the available clear 'lanes' in advance of needing them."

Phase three (ii): risk management

"I clearly remember my most perfect junior race: after a finely timed pin end start, we tacked onto port across the fleet to hit the favoured starboard layline. We led at the first mark by 100 yards and won the race by a mile. The sort of race we all dream about… Unless sailing against substandard competition, or with an indecent boat speed advantage, this does not happen six in a row. The risk of unexpected wind shifts, or other phenomena, actually makes it more likely that by the time we achieve our dream result, we are out of the championship running because we already have two discards!"

Except possibly when handicap sailing (chapter 12), sailing is not just a race against the clock. A race win by a boat length is the same result as a win by a leg. To win a race, we don't have to win every leg. To win a regatta, we don't have to win every race.

With any strategy there is an element of risk. Generally, the bigger the potential gain, the bigger the risk. For example, Ryan's strategy in his dream race was "Let's get onto port early, and not tack back onto starboard until we can lay the windward mark." This sounds fine if his wind prediction is guaranteed, but what if the fleet had read the conditions differently and stayed to the left of the course? He won by a huge margin by getting it right. But if he had missed something with his weather prediction, he could have been last by an equally huge margin, with no chance to get back in the race.

A safe compromise would be to favour the right but remain in touch with the fleet. If the prediction is correct, he still makes his gain, but if it's wrong he is still in touch.

"I'm thinking about my exposure. If most of the fleet is sailing the same direction, there is probably a reason for it. I may have to split far enough to get clear wind after a bad start. But if they are right and we're wrong, splitting is more likely to let them get further away. Instead I shadow the pack and concentrate on making small gains on shifts, boat speed and boat handling through the race to get back among them.

"My rule is, match the risk to my goal. If all I need to do to win a championship is finish in the top 10 in every race, there is no need to be exposed right at the edge of the course or the fleet."

"Positioning": the next section of this chapter suggests basic strategies for sailing a beat in uncertain conditions. If we are absolutely confident of our strategic assets, we can largely ignore these rules until we get close to the layline: we just sail the fastest course, irrespective of the fleet geometry. At the other end of the scale, in completely uncertain conditions the only strategy we have is that of positioning. For every beat of every race, there is a balance between sailing the fastest course, and positioning against the fleet. We choose our balance point based on the confidence we have that our strategic priorities are correct.

"Hopefully I have now convinced you that working out a strategy and banging the corners may be fun every now and then, but it's not a formula for consistent success. My risk management strategy, or 'winning formula' is steady accumulation, and that's where positioning comes into the equation".

Tack, dip, or call?

Off the start, we need clear wind. So there is no point completing a perfect lee bow tack if it forces us back into an area of dirty wind. Better to dip some transoms and get clear air as soon as possible.

Once clear, we are aiming to follow our strategy. If we are on port and want to go right, ducking a starboard boat is going to get us there more quickly than a lee bow tack. If we tack we'll have to wait until the other boat tacks off. If we are on starboard and trying to go left, waving a port boat past will help us to achieve our objectives more quickly. If we want to be free to tack with the oscillations, or we are not confident that we can make a lee bow tack stick, tacking a couple of boat lengths to leeward of the approaching boat leaves us with all the options, and preempts an aggressive lee bow tack from the other boat (fig 7.8).

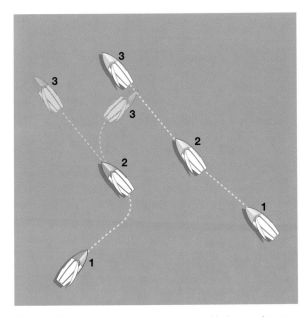

Fig: 7.8 *Orange tacks safely to leeward. He is now free to continue on starboard, or tack at will. If he'd tried a lee bow, he'd be stuck on starboard until Yellow peeled off.*

A perfect lee bow tack is pointless if the other boat simply sails us to the layline. If on starboard there is no need to lose a nice lane when covering the pack back to the middle of the course, by allowing a port boat to make an aggressive lee bow tack and force us back out to the starboard side of the course. If possible, we wave the port tacker past. He'll probably return the favour next time.

"From any crossing situation on the windward mark approach we should make the call which is most likely to give us the controlling situation.

"The decision we make when we meet a boat on the other tack should not be made 'off the cuff'. We must think 'big picture', and make sure a crossing boat does not distract us from this."

Options for the port boat

Use the lee bow tack:
* If the starboard boat is going where we want to go.
* We want his lane.
* We are confident that we are far enough advanced that he will not roll us as we complete the tack.

Don't use the lee bow:
* If we think we may want an early tack back to port.
* If there are a lot more port boats level and to our left lining up to do exactly the same to us.
* If we want to encourage the starboard boat to keep coming the same way where we can keep an eye on him! In this case, use the safe leeward tack.

Use the safe leeward tack (fig 7.8):
* If we like the look of the starboard boat's line.
* We expect a port header soon.
* We want to be able to tack back at will.
* We are not confident that we are far enough forward to pull off a good lee bow tack.

A safe leeward tack gets us going in the right direction without losing ground through ducking or limiting our options for the future. However, if there are lots more boats level and stacked up on our port quarter, it may be better to duck the starboard boat and tack safely to windward. This way he acts as a blocker from any of these boats which threaten to ruin everything with a lee bow tack.

Dip: In a well executed dip, the extra speed gained reduces the distance lost considerably.

Use the dip:
• If we are going the right way.
• We are close to the port layline.
• We are not confident that we'll pull off a lee bow and there is too much traffic to the left for a safe leeward tack.

"As the boats get bigger, a good dip requires more practice; it's a real team effort. What should be a 20 ft dip in a keelboat can easily become a 60 ft one if the manoeuvre is not perfect. In that case there is no point bothering: you may as well tack every time."

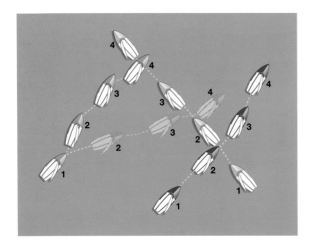

Fig: 7.9 *The alternative dip. Rather than bearing away, Orange sails high and slow, moving away from any lee bow effect from Purple*

In fig 7.9, Orange uses the alternative dip. He really does not want to tack, but if he ducks Pink, he'll start to get bad air from Purple. Instead, he sails really high and slow, effectively waiting for Pink to reach him. He'll duck, but keep his lane. Orange could also use this move to close the gap on a boat to windward and achieve a lee bow position.

Photo 7.1 *A perfect alternative dip opportunity. 082 could have avoided bearing off into 088's lee bow by sailing high and slow for 4 boat lengths*

Options for the starboard boat

Carry on call:

"There are far more 'carry on' calls at the front of any fleet than there are at the back. There must be a reason for this."

At the beginning of a leg, the last thing the front runners want to do is to get involved with an individual while the rest of the fleet sail away. As soon as it is clear that two boats are converging on opposite tacks, a good sailor will make a judgment: "will he cross? will he be able to lee bow me? if he tacks will we just roll over him?" If the answer to the first or second questions is "yes", and the starboard boat has no reason to tack, "carry on" is the right call.

"To avoid last minute surprises, make sure that the call is clear, and acknowledged by the other boat. Then move into a smooth and fast duck to reduce any loss to a minimum." (photo 7.2 page 91)

"Starboard!". Putting the other boat about is fine if we are far enough advanced to roll over them when they tack, or if we were planning to tack in any case. But if we really don't want to tack, a "carry on" call may be more appropriate.

"Go right". There are two ways to go right for the boat on starboard tack. A lee bow tack is tricky: it's difficult to achieve this without fouling the port tack boat, as the port boat will start bearing away to dip before we need to begin our tack.

A safe leeward tack (a mirror image of Orange's tack in fig 7.8 page 87) is the soft option. The "slam dunk" (fig 7.10) is a possibility. This only works with relatively heavy boats which keep their way through the tack. It will definitely not work in a performance dinghy: the slam dunker will at best be lee bowed, and at worst on the way to the protest room.

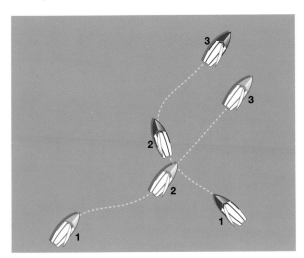

Fig 7.10 The "slam dunk": practise this first!

 "Don't try the slam dunk out in anger without practising first; it's easy to get wrong!"

Duck, tack or wave: some questions to ask in advance:

- Can I cross?
- Will he cross?
- Which way do I want to go?
- Where is the majority of the fleet?
- Will the next shift be a lift or a header?
- How much distance are we going to give away?
- How close are we to the layline?

I'm thinking about ducking:

- If we duck the first boat will there be more to duck afterwards?
- Will we be able to find a lane or will we have to sail all the way to the right?
- What does the traffic to windward on starboard look like?

I'm thinking about tacking:

- Do I want to send the other boat off on starboard?
- How quickly will we make the lee bow stick: will the other boat tack off straight away or will it be a long hard grind?
- Are there lots more port boats further left? Would I be better passing astern, tacking on his hip, and using him as a blocker?

I'm thinking about calling the other boat past ("waving"):

- Are there more boats after this one: will I have to keep ducking and ducking, or are there so many that one is bound to go for a lee bow?

Phase four: what is happening?

"Once a third to half way up the beat, it's usually pretty clear whether our strategy is working. Conditions change. We don't always get our predictions right. In the boat, we talk about what is happening, who is gaining, and why. We look for more indications, such as other fleets on the same course, or weather clues. If we have got the strategy wrong, we change it now, take our medicine, and get back into the race. If we have got it right, we look at consolidating, and setting up for a good windward mark approach."

Keep them behind

As the beat develops, we may be in the fortunate situation of having only one or two close competitors. One tactic is to move directly into defensive mode, but this can be counter productive. The covered boat may go the wrong way, allowing the bulk of the fleet to pull back, presenting more of a challenge on the run. And we lose any real opportunity to turn a small lead into a convincing one which would make the rest of the race less stressful.

"In the first race of our nationals, three quarters of the way up the first beat, we were leading the fleet. As we started to tack, I realised we'd be right on the wind of our most likely close competitor for the championship - at this time he was fighting for clear air, back in the pack. That tack led to one of the most acrimonious regattas I have ever sailed! We won the race, but our aggressive tactics gave him the extra determination to win the regatta. In this instance, a close cover had definitely not been the most effective way to protect our position."

We'll discuss more aggressive defensive techniques in chapter 13. The standard rules for consolidating a position, and defending a lead on the first beat use the basic positional themes: use the oscillating shifts to reduce the chasing boats' leverage, working towards a position between the leading pack and the windward mark, and avoiding sailing outside the "shift lines". (More on p84)

Coming from behind

As suggested in chapter 7, splitting from the bulk of the fleet is rarely a good idea: there is usually a good reason that they have gone that way.

"Taking a flier to the opposite side of the course works about one time in every 50: the problem is that our selective memory always remembers that one. Don't forget: if we are directly downwind of a boat ahead, we can gain whichever way the wind shifts."

Once we've found a lane of clear wind, we have to be prepared for the long haul, looking at passing boats a few at a time, making small gains through shifts or wind patches on the favoured side of the course. Our objective is not necessarily to get back to our rightful position in the second half of the beat; it is to minimize the distance from the leaders, giving us an achievable target for the rest of the race. (More in chapter 13)

Phase five: Controlling the approach

We'll look at specifics in the second part of this chapter. In uncertain conditions, we'd ideally lead the fleet back in towards the rhumb line. In a wind bend, we'd aim to time our tack so we get lifted up to the mark, rather than sailing extra distance. We certainly don't want to be stuck in the leebow of another boat, with the choice of sailing slowly or tacking off and overstanding.

"Making the final approach well below the layline is even more important when back in the pack. Once I get there the only way to keep clear wind is to tack just beyond the boats in front. Of course, they did the same to the boats in front of them! So we either get gassed or over stand, big time!" (see photo 'windward 1')

Phase six: the approach

As the windward mark looms, boat on boat tactics become increasingly important. Objectives in the final sector include: preparing a winning offwind strategy; maintaining clear wind without overstanding; putting space on the boats immediately behind to give clear air for the offwind leg; and taking advantage of mistakes from the boats ahead. We'll cover this part of the beat in chapter 8.

The beat 2: Positioning

Photo 7.2

"It's the first race of Kiel Week, 2004. The wind is offshore, and there does not seem to be any real pattern to the oscillations, or any other significant natural asset. With 15 minutes to the start, I have six young and enthusiastic 420 sailors asking my advice: 'which way'? As a sailor, I'd 'make the best of a bad job' in these conditions: concentrate on the factors I can control - boat speed, boat handling, start well - and then just... sail by feel: that usually works! But there is some science to 'sailing by feel' in confusing 'none of the above' conditions. Dr. Stuart Walker calls this science 'positioning'."

When conditions are uncertain, we'll be lucky to find the absolutely shortest or fastest route around the race course. Everyone is bound to miss a few shifts. Positioning relative to the other boats becomes the overriding concept.

What do we mean by leverage?

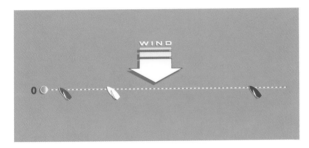

Fig: 7.11 Three boats equally progressed towards the wind

The "line of equality" at right angles to the wind direction passes through each of Red, White, and Blue's masts. (This is the theoretical line painted on the water in the America's Cup sailings TV coverage!). Therefore they are equally progressed up the beat, towards the wind (fig 7.11). Red is separated from White by 2 boat lengths, with a further eight boat lengths to Blue.

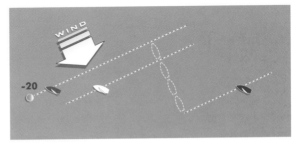

Fig: 7.12 The wind heads, Red gains one boat length over White, who gains 3 boat lengths over Blue

Imagine an instantaneous header of 20 degrees (fig 7.12): the boats are still in the same positions, but they have had to bear away by the same amount. We have all been in Blue's position: suddenly the boats we were level with have popped out in front of our jib. Though the boats have not moved through the water, the wind shift has given an advantage to Red. Look at the size of the gain: Red has gained one boat length directly to windward (almost a boat and a half in real sailing distance) on White. The gain is four boat lengths to windward on Blue.

"The boats have not moved, but the windshift has given a significant gain."

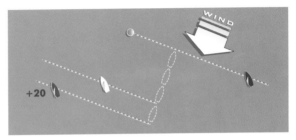

Fig: 7.13 The wind lifts, and the situation is reversed

Now look at an instantaneous lift of 20 degrees (fig 7.13): Blue has gained three boat lengths on White, and four on Red.

Photo 7.3 *The larger the sideways separation, the greater the leverage. That means a bigger gain or loss from a shift*

"In both cases, the amount gained is proportional to the distance between the boats. Doubling the separation from a boat, or bunch of boats, doubles the distance we stand to lose or gain from a shift. That's why we call it leverage. So if I want to make a big gain I will split further from the fleet. I will only do this if I am willing to risk a big loss, or am very sure about the next shift. If I'm not so confident, I'll edge towards my favoured side but reduce the leverage over my closest competitors." (photo 7.3)

Note that this gain due to a wind shift is a "paper gain". If the wind shifts back, the relative positions revert. It's only consolidated when we actually cross ahead of the boats concerned: once we are directly upwind of a competitor, there is no leverage, the loss due to a wind shift is small: the money is in the bank! (fig 7.15)

A similar principle applies to sideways separation from the fleet when other natural

assets are prevalent. A big separation implies maximum benefit from more wind, less tide, or a wind bend. It also exposes us to more risk, should practice not match theory.

Increasing leverage

With medium to large sized fleets, most boats start on starboard, and continue on starboard until they've gained a big enough advantage on the boats around to tack and clear. The bigger the fleet, the longer this takes; there is usually a big line of starboard boats all trying to do the same. Boats in the second rank which tack and cross behind the first row are often ignored: they are already several boat lengths behind. Some boats may have started at the starboard end of the line, and tacked directly onto port tack. That's fine if the starboard tackers are sailing on a high starboard number, or towards the advantaged left side.

But a boat which starts ten boat lengths up the line and tacks directly onto port tack could have 50 boat lengths separation after a minute. (fig 7.14) A right shift of just 8 degrees would give the boat on the right a gain of around 5 boat lengths: the second row starters who tacked behind look quite good now!

"We may not be concerned about individual boats if we are controlling the majority, but if it's us splitting from the fleet on a bad compass number we have to be aware that our exposure is increasing - and quickly!"

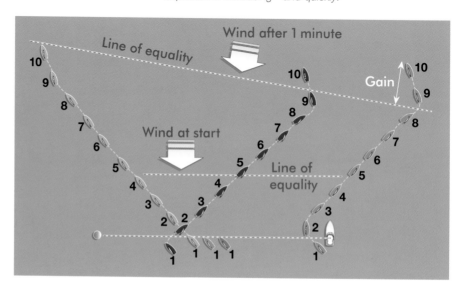

7.14 Orange tacks immediately around the committee boat. Pink continues on starboard. After just a minute, there is sufficient leverage for a significant gain from a windshift.

Banking the header

In oscillating conditions, a wind shift gain isn't fully realised until we physically cross the competition. Until then, a shift the other way would negate the gain. Purple consolidates the gain from the header, by tacking to cross ahead of Pink. If the wind shifts either way, his gain is safe (fig 7.15).

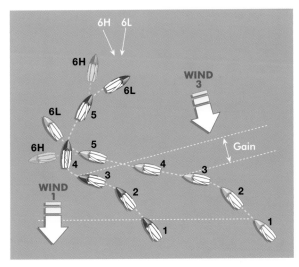

Fig 7.15 Purple makes a "paper gain" when the wind heads. He can now tack and cross. Now the wind can lift or head (positions 6H and 6L) and his gain remains safe

If Pink believes that the next shift will be a port header, her attacking move is to tack onto port with Purple. This would prevent Purple from consolidating, and set Pink up for a gain when the next starboard shift comes.

Photo 7.4 334 tacks to "bank" the gain made through the header

Banking the lift

How does Orange consolidate in the big lift? (fig 7.16) If all the boats continue as they are, an equivalent header will negate his gain. Tacking would make it worse.

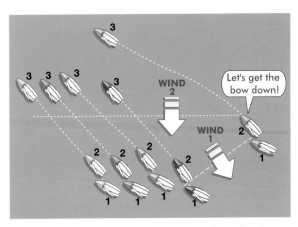

Fig 7.16 Orange banks the gain from a lift by sailing fast and free

"I love this bit! There is only one way to put a lift in the bank! Sail fast and free. Even 'lead mines' go slightly faster when sailed free. A trapeze boat goes at double speed. All I have to do is turn the windward height I have gained through the wind shift into forward distance. The leverage reduces, and I actually move forward compared with the boats to leeward."

Decreasing exposure

But we don't have to put it all in the bank. Orange feels there is some natural advantage from the right hand side of the course, but there are also significant oscillations (fig 7.17). Though she's already the furthest right boat, in a drag race she'd keep going closer to the edge. She takes the conservative approach, using a large port header to take a hitch back towards the pack. She has reduced her exposure, but retains control of the favoured side (fig 7.17).

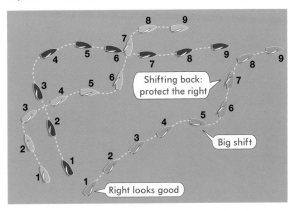

Fig 7.17 Orange uses a right hand shift to reduce her exposure, but keeps to the right of the fleet, maintaining control of her favoured side

Laylines

Once we have reached either layline, any shift gives an advantage to the boats inside the layline (fig 7.18). A lift (position 2) gives no advantage as it's still the same distance for Pink to sail to the windward mark, and Yellow will now lay the mark, sailing less distance. A header (position 3) leaves Pink pointing at the fleet's transoms: yellow can simply tack and cross ahead.

Fig 7.18 With no other influences, a boat on the layline loses if there is a shift

On the larger scale the layline is even more significant (fig 7.19). Pink is exposed on the left, approaching the layline, lifted on starboard. She does not want to tack. She's relieved that the header comes before she reaches the layline, but she still sails more distance than Orange who can now sail straight to the mark.

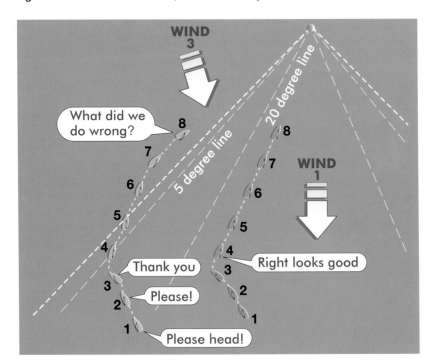

Fig 7.19 Though Pink is inside the layline, she has passed the "shift line" the layline created when the wind shifts left. Once past the shift line on either side of the course, a shift in either direction will disadvantage Pink

"When the shifts are unpredictable and we are well inside the layline, we can wait for the favourable shift before tacking. If we are close to the layline, there is less chance of it arriving. We'll either have to tack and sail on a heading shift simply because we have reached the layline, or like Pink, sail extra distance (compared with Orange who stayed inside the shift line) through hanging on and hoping."

It is pretty clear that if the wind is shifting through 5 degrees, sailing outside the 5 degree "shift line" will probably incur extra distance. If 20 degrees, the shift line is at 20 degrees. The earlier we get close to these "no go" areas, the bigger the potential loss. The closer we get, the less time there is for the wind to shift in our favour.

Long leg first

"I know successful sailors who only have one strategy: 'bow forward on the longest tack!'"

This is the logical extension to the layline strategy. If the beat is significantly biased, the boats sailing on the short leg are fast approaching the layline. Once close to the layline, any shift will give a gain to the boats on the long leg. If in fig 7.19, the start of the beat had been with the boats in position 1, Orange's early tack onto port would give her the controlling position on the long tack.

Herding

Though all fleets have their "two tack" specialists, on the water we can often influence group dynamics. By gently pushing a couple of boats in the direction we want to go, we can control the group, preventing them increasing leverage while encouraging them to sail towards our favoured side.

Orange feels the header, and sees boats below peeling back to the centre of the course. He sits out hard, sets the boat up for pointing, and turns his safe leeward position into a lee bow, forcing Pink to tack. Once Pink and Orange have tacked, Green and Grey will likely follow (fig 7.20).

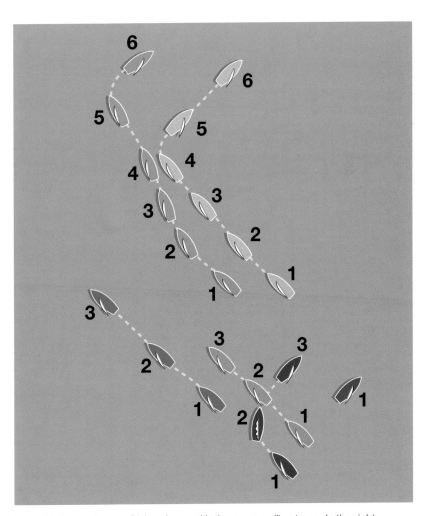

Fig 7.20 *Orange forces Pink to keep with the group sailing towards the right*

Mauve sails fast and free, down onto Green's wind. Green has to tack. Now Mauve tacks back, parallel with Green: he'll give her clear wind until he wants her to tack again! (fig 7.21)

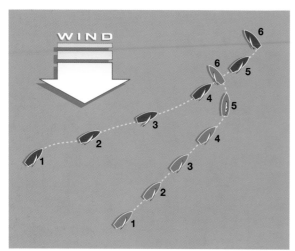

Fig 7.21 Mauve sails onto Green's wind to encourage her to tack

Win a side

"Sometimes I really can't work out which way the wind will shift next, or whether some other strategic asset will make a difference. One solution is to pick a side, and aim to use positioning gains to win it"

If neither tack is lifted, the beat is square, and there is no significant line bias, we might choose the side that our major competition, the local hot shot, or simply the majority of the fleet is heading. This way we'll still be in the race at the windward mark, and hopefully we'll have learned enough on the first beat to start the next one better informed!

Turn theory into practice

In uncertain conditions we can divide the beat into three phases:
• Gain
• Consolidate
• Look for opportunities

Make the gain

However difficult the conditions, if we want to win we have to expose ourselves and gain an advantage at some stage; if we tack all the way up the rhumb line we'll have no lead to consolidate! Layline discussions on page 94 suggest that this move should be made at the start of the beat, before the course starts to narrow: if we make a mistake there is more time to put it right, if we are waiting for the header there is more time for it to arrive before we hit the "shift line".

"To make a gain, increase leverage"

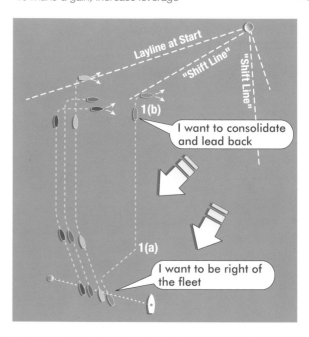

Fig 7.22 Expecting the right shift, Orange makes his move to the right early in the beat. When the boats on his left tack onto port, he tacks to lead back into the course

"Scenario 1 (fig 7.22): I think the wind is going to lift on starboard. I need to be on the right hand side of the pack. I either need to be able to tack early and cross the pack, or start near the starboard end. If the starboard heading is low, and I'm very confident of the port lift, I can tack right off the start line. Once the right hand shift comes, if still on port, I tack back onto starboard. I can put the bow down and bank some of the gain if I think it is short term, if not I just keep going toward the layline. Once we get close to the layline, the boats further left will have to tack, and we'll have consolidated our gain."

"If it heads while I am to windward, I don't need to tack immediately: the boats to leeward don't consolidate until they tack and cross. I minimise risk, wait for them, tack below and bow forward, and lead towards the next right shift. When that comes, I can tack and cross most of the boats, consolidating my gain." (fig 7.23)

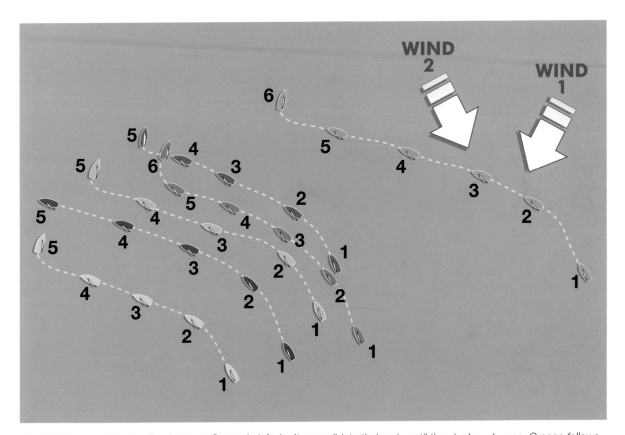

Fig 7.23 *The wind heads. The boats to Orange's left don't consolidate their gain until they tack and cross. Orange follows them to the left: he does not want to increase the leverage in case the wind moves further left. He tacks when they do, leading back into the course. If Orange in position 3 felt that the wind would move further left, he could have reduced leverage by sailing free*

"Scenario 2 (fig 7.24): The wind is right of the mean. Even if there is an initial lift, I think there is time for the wind to move left before we reach the layline. My start strategy must enable me to keep going on starboard: I don't want to tack! If the wind does lift more, I can use this to move forward on any boats to leeward: I want to lead into my left hand shift! In fact the wind does begin to head. Though I'm expecting more, some boats tack. I'm well away from the shift line, I'm not exposed to a lot of boats on the right, as I'm confident that there is more to come, I keep going until all the boats on the left have tacked."

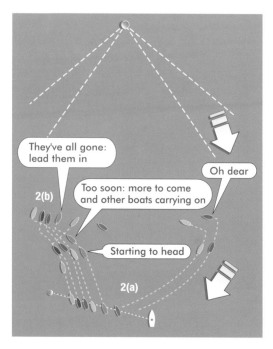

Fig 7.24 *Orange pushes to his expected favoured side in the first part of the beat*

"If I am going to take some risk to gain an advantage, I do it in the first part of the beat: if I've missed something from my strategy, I may have a chance to put that right, and if I'm waiting for a shift, there is more time before I reach the 'shift line'."

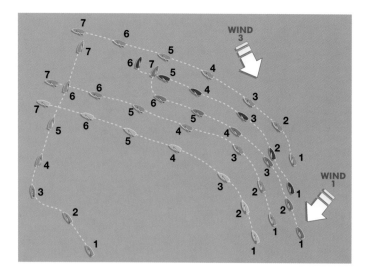

Fig 7.25 *Orange switches from "gain" to "consolidate" mode*

Consolidate

We'll look at recovery tactics in chapter 13. For now we'll assume that we have some gains over the pack to consolidate.

"Now I want to consolidate my gains, get closer to the mass of the fleet, and unless there is a definite gain out there, keep away from the shift lines."

"I'm in Orange, in fig 7.25. I've made my gain on the left hand side of the course. It's time to switch to consolidation mode: I tack on the next header, cross the majority of the fleet, to my left and lead back into the centre of the course."

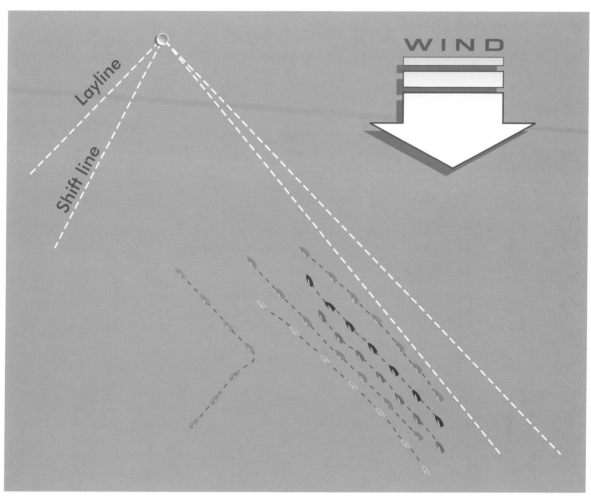

Fig 7.26 *Orange tacks ahead and to leeward keeping all options open*

"Some of the boats from the right hand side are slightly ahead, but close to the shift line. There are no clear lanes without sailing all the way to the outside of the course. In consolidation mode I don't want to do this. I tack ahead and to leeward giving maximum opportunity to gain on the last few shifts to the mark." (fig 7.26)

Look for opportunities

As the mark gets closer, a gain as small as 1 metre could turn into a position. We'll look at this phase of the beat in chapter 8.

The "mass" of the fleet

Who do we mean when we are talking about "the pack" or "the fleet"? Certainly not any back markers who are happy to set off in the opposite direction to everyone in the quest for the "lucky shift" which they find once or twice a year. And, if we are mid fleet, not the group of boats too far away to reasonably hope to catch on this leg. We mean the group of boats we are racing with on this leg. At the start of the first beat, this is probably the whole fleet. As the race develops it may settle down to 5 or 10 boats, or the race may be so closely congested that only a few drop out of the back.

Where is "the pack" when everyone splits in different directions? Now we have to make a judgement call. If we are on the lifted tack - along with part of the fleet - and we are confident that we'll get a significant header before the layline, "the pack" is the group of boats coming our way. If the closest competition - or the hot locals - are going one way they are probably "the pack". If the fleet is totally split and there is no way to call which is the most threatening group of boats (ahead or behind) then our positioning in the fleet has to be against "the mass": a sort of weighted average position, a centre of gravity. The question we are looking to answer is: where is the mass and which way is it moving?

We are still in the race!

The first boat at the windward mark may not have used a conservative positioning strategy, but unless he is exceptionally fast, or he knows something that we don't about the conditions, he won't be first every time.

 "The less confident we are of the prevailing natural assets, the more important these positioning principles become. And once we have made our move to the favoured side, or got in phase with the oscillations, we can use the same concepts to consolidate an advantage over the other boats around."

The best chance of achieving the consistent results needed to win a series comes from the conservative accumulation process:

- Make the most of every small gain.
- Consolidate at every opportunity.
- Put the boat in the position most likely to create the next opportunity.

Further reading

Positioning: The Logic Of Sailboat Racing
Stuart H Walker (now out of print but lots of
second-hand copies available).

The windward mark

"Approaching the spacer mark at the Laser SB3 Europeans in Lake Garda, we are in the top 10 of a fleet of 60. Just as the right hand side paid on the beat, with more pressure and a wind bend under the cliffs, we are expecting that the left will pay on the run. In anticipation, we have rigged the kite on the starboard side, ready for a gybe set. The boat ahead starts to bear away, and slows. We have to luff to avoid wiping out his backstay with our already set pole. As we do so, we see that his kite is rigged on the port side: that could be an issue.

"He hoists as he bears away: a slow one. We are now fully overlapped on his starboard side. 'Come on: gybe!'

"As his spinnaker finally fills, he accelerates away and breaks the overlap. We are at last clear to gybe and set our kite. Just as we do, the boat behind executes a perfect gybe set: right on our wind! He's exactly where we wanted to be. We're now in the slow lane, with no slip road in sight."

If we are to use the mark approach as a springboard into the next leg, we need all three parts of the equation:
- Plan.
- Preparation.
- Execution.

Sometimes the execution may have to change in response to an unexpected move from the boat ahead or behind; and occasionally the plan has to change too. However, once committed to a manoeuvre such as the gybe set described above, our first priority must be to position our boat to enable the execution of the plan.

In the final sector of the beat we are looking to:
- Decide the offwind plan and round the mark in good shape to execute this strategy.
- Consolidate any advantage over the opposition, and, if possible, put space between us and the boats around to give clear wind on the next leg.
- Keep clear wind for as long as possible.
- Use boat on boat tactics to make the most of developing opportunities.

"Let's first look at some general principles which affect the way we line up for the final approach, then develop these into classic windward mark situations and how to make the best of them."

Offwind strategy

In chapter 6 we used the start as the springboard to launch into our upwind strategy. In exactly the same way, we can look at the windward mark as the springboard for the offwind strategy.

 "As we've seen above, there is no point rounding the windward mark outside a bunch of boats if we want to gybe set! If it's a broad-ish reach with puffs coming down from the right, I really want to try to generate a gap behind so I can hook into these puffs then use them to soak, without being threatened by boats behind and to windward. If it's a tight reach and I want to go high initially before setting the kite, there is no point tacking on the buoy inside a bunch of boats unless I'm sure to pop out clear ahead. If I am overlapped to leeward the chances are, even if I try to luff, they'll reach over the top while hoisting their kites leaving me struggling to get to my course through bad wind and water."

The layline

Unless there is a clear tidal or wind pressure advantage right out to one side, hitting the lay line early rarely pays. Here are three reasons:

Strategic (fig 8.1)

Orange and Pink are equally advanced up the course (positions 1,2,3). The wind heads 20 degrees (4H). Orange is now ahead, can and will tack and cross Pink, and lead to the mark. If the wind had lifted 20 degrees (4L), Orange would now lay the mark and again round inside and ahead of Pink. Both lift and header disadvantage Pink who hit the layline too early, and the same principle would apply to boats which over or under estimate the tide: the later the layline decision, the less potential for loss.

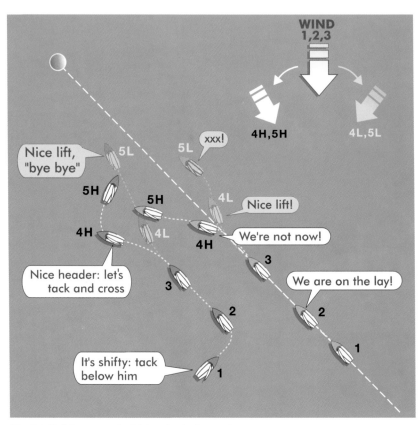

***Fig 8.1** Pink loses out by hitting the layline early*

Tactical (fig 8.2)

Orange and Mauve are equally advanced up the course. Mauve has shown her cards early by tacking on the lay line. Her early commitment gives Orange a great indication of just where the lay line is. If Mauve's sheets are eased, it's a pretty good indication she is over the layline. Orange can use this to control the approach. In this case Mauve has judged the layline spot on. Orange simply tacks to lee bow Yellow, squeezes up to lay the mark comfortably and leads Mauve around. If the wind heads, neither will lay, but Orange will gain more from the lee bow and will be ahead when they both tack. If the wind lifts, both will lay the mark, Orange will round inside and ahead. (See fig 8.6 p109 for ways for Mauve to defend from Orange in this situation.)

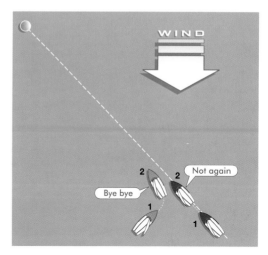

Fig 8.2 *Orange simply tacks and leebows Mauve, leading into the mark*

Clear wind (fig 8.3)

Orange has sailed a perfect beat, there is no cross tide and shifts are small so he's confident that they can judge the layline. With no close threat from the left hand side, Orange is happy that there is no exposure on the layline. Mauve saw the jam stacking up, and avoided the bad air zone, making his final port tack approach to the lay line 3 or 4 boat lengths below the layline, and looking for the right boat starboard to tack underneath. To be safe from Rule 18.3 he completes this tack outside the 2 boat lengths zone. He has moved from "also ran" to a secure second place, through finding a lane with clear wind, and avoiding the lay line, passing Yellow who has tacked in clear wind behind and to windward: sacrificing extra distance for clear wind. Red, also wanting clear wind, in turn tacks behind and to windward of Yellow, and as the situation develops, the traffic jam ("the slow lane") builds. Now Green finds a way to sniddle through the starboard tackers, and tacks, right on Red's wind. Red is already overstanding so can't tack off. As each new boat comes across to the layline, it is forced to overstand more to get clear wind on the approach, giving more bad wind to the boats behind. Orange's smiles get bigger and bigger!

Fig 8.3 *Mauve avoids layline misery by using a late port approach*

"In Orange's position now I'd start to really turn the screw: I'd sail high, heel the boat to windward, and make the pack really suffer. At three or so boat lengths from the mark, I'd reach off and trim for speed, aiming to hit full reaching speed with the kite 'made' just as we bear away round the mark, leaving our competitors wallowing in their accumulated bad air.

"The leaders have few concerns over dirty wind on the layline. The more boats there are ahead, the worse the effect. So if I'm further down the pack, I'll tack well below the layline to minimise time sailed in wind shadow without sailing extra distance."

When approaching the windward mark in a big pack, the safe choices often appear to be: "sail past the starboard layline until you reach a clear lane to windward" (Green), or "tack on the layline and take your medicine" (Pink). But by watching the patterns develop, looking for the gaps, and avoiding the layline as late as possible, it's possible to turn a mediocre rounding into an acceptable one. To do this we need the boat handling and rules skill to match!

How do we judge the layline?

Sadly the laylines shown on the diagrams are not as clearly drawn in real life. It's possible to pick up a transit on a practice beat (but be aware of windshifts), and to get hints from fleets ahead. Be aware of any tidal effect, in particular there are always many boat lengths gained and lost on the first beat when there is a strong favourable tide. As with most sailing skills, practice improves accuracy. Leaving the layline approach to three or four boat lengths makes all these judgments less critical.

If tide is significant, tacking on the leader's line won't work even if the leader has it spot on: if she is half as far from the mark, she's only got half as much time in the fair or foul tide!

Photo 8.1 *Each boat in turn overstands a little more to maintain clear wind to the mark. This leaves plenty of opportunities for gains from the left*

"The leader often gives a good clue to the layline, you can see whether he has overstood and easing sheets or struggling to lay the mark. However the classic 'let's sail behind his transom and see if she is laying' is a sure fire way to join the great circle route and give away distance: if he has overstood, we've done even worse!"

Pink sights down Orange's centreline as she crosses behind (fig 8.4). Orange appears three boat lengths below the layline. Tacking now would already be too late: with twice as much distance to the mark, the tide will take her twice as far to windward as Orange. In any case, Orange is not below the layline: she has correctly compensated for the tide, and is laying comfortably. Meanwhile Mauve tacks on his layline, well before reaching Orange's line, and leaves Pink to sail her great circle route!

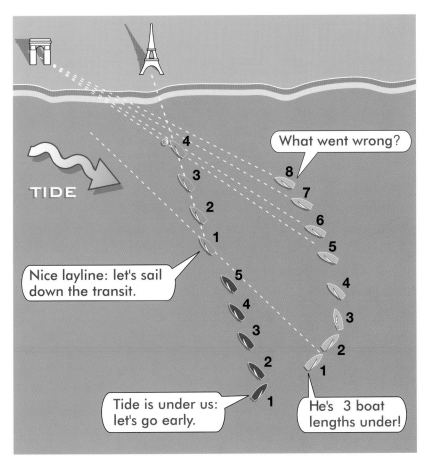

Using the transit

Once committed to the final approach, the transit enables us to establish that we are actually laying the mark, and to sail the straight line course if we have overstood. In fig 8.4, Orange and Mauve have picked up a fabulous landmark right in line with the windward mark. If the tower stays in line with the windward mark, they are sailing the straight line route. If the tower appears to moves to the **right** compared with the mark, they are overstanding, they need to ease sheets and bear away (turning **left**!). If the land is moving **left**, they are underlaying the mark, and need to "turn **right**" to sail the straight line course. At point 5, Pink would have seen the Arc moving hard right! She could have minimised her loss and sailed the straight line course from that point to the mark by bearing away until the Arc stayed directly behind the mark.

Fig 8.4 *The tide magnifies Pink's misjudgement: sighting through Orange's line has given a completely misleading picture*

Which approach?

When racing on a big course with a small fleet, or even a well spread big one, strategic considerations take precedence over "boat on boat" tactical ones. The best gains come from sailing the fastest route to the windward mark, and using the moves below to deal with the other boats. If the oscillations are such that the final lifted approach will be on port tack, there may be a significant gain from approaching on port.

However, typically in a big, closely matched fleet, the windward mark area is so congested that there is simply no way through on port. "Keep cool" (fig 8.7 p111) may help, but a close port tack approach is risky. In this case the only solution is to commit to joining the "slow lane", on starboard tack, work hard at finding a suitable gap, as clear wind as possible, and with as small an overstand as is necessary to give a reasonable line to the mark.

 "You will gather from this that I am not a great fan of the layline! The ideal time to hit the starboard layline, other variables permitting, is at a distance which gives sufficient time to prepare pole and spinnaker for launch at the mark, and get mainsheet, kicker, and Cunningham controls ready to ease for the bear away. Once on starboard, I double check that we are laying taking account of tide and leeway, then use the moves below to defend from port tack predators."

Approaching on port

The port tack approach puts increased pressure on boat handling. It requires accurate tacking, and reliable acceleration. An ability to turn the boat quickly at slow speed, with a quick sort of spinnaker gear for a hoist immediately out of the tack and bear-away is a bonus. It needs great anticipation skills to find the right gap, and also requires that any starboard tackers interpret the racing rules just as we do!

 "The port tack approach is a favourite when leading a race: it's really satisfying to watch the competition slowing each other in a line above the starboard layline while we sail to the mark at full speed, tack, and disappear! Further down the fleet, especially when there are visible gaps, it can be a way to keep clear wind right to the end of the beat and recover places at the end of a bad beat (photos 8.2, 8.4). However, watch out for boats already on their way down the first offwind leg! And if a long way back in a big fleet, watch out for the wind shadow below the leading pack, especially if there is a spacer mark.

Points to remember when using the port tack approach:

- Be absolutely clear on the meaning of Rule 18.3.

- Be aware of any tidal effect and allow for this to prevent overstanding or understanding the mark.

- Don't begin a port tack approach so close below another boat that he'll stop you tacking back onto starboard at will.

- If the layline is congested, or there is doubt as to whether a starboard tacker is laying, it's safer to dip or cross clear ahead and tack to windward, than to attempt a lee bow.

- If there is a spacer mark before the real offwind leg proper, don't tack to leeward of another starboard tack boat unless you are certain to achieve at least a lee bow position. If one boat rolls past on the fetch to the spacer mark, more will follow.

- And don't try this in anger without practising all these skills first!

Photo 8.2 GBR 406 avoids the great circle route by approaching late on port

Photo 8.3 He ducks bow number 38

Photo 8.4 There is now space for him to tack between 52 and 38. He'll be close hauled well before 52 has to make any alteration. Even if he were tacking at 2 boat lengths, 52 is 25 degrees off close hauled so would not have to luff above close hauled to keep clear

Boat on boat tactics

We have decided how we want to play the offwind leg. From this we can plan our optimum positioning against the other boats at the windward mark. We have made the best of the final wind shifts and clear lanes, and know what the tidal situation is at the windward mark. Here are 6 boat on boat "sniddles", we can use to gain and maintain optimum positioning.

Disguise the layline

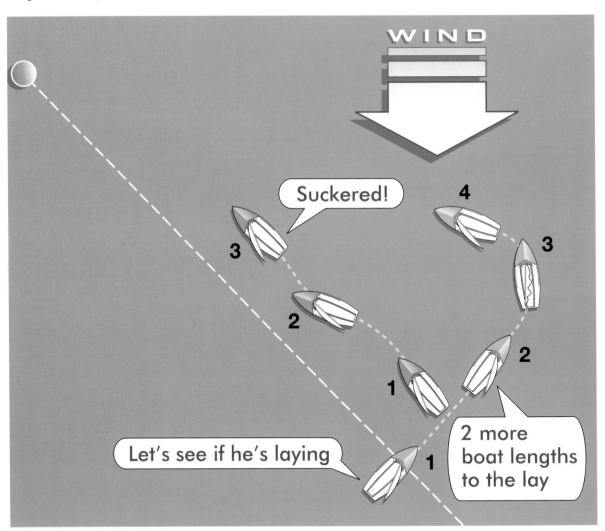

Fig 8.5 *Orange gains breathing space by persuading Pink to overstand*

"I'm in Orange, but have overlaid a bit. If I can persuade Pink to overstand the mark the same distance or more, I'll gain distance and have more chance of clear wind on the offwind leg. So as she comes close to my line, I gently bear away. When she sights through my transom, it appears that I am below the layline. With luck she'll sail another four or five boat lengths before she realises!"

Repel boarders

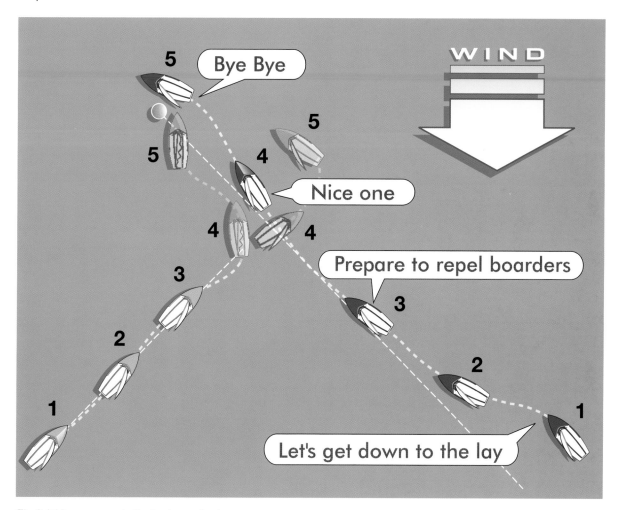

Fig 8.6 *Mauve prevents the lee bow attack*

"I am Mauve, above the layline. I really don't want a port tack approacher to lee bow me and lead in to the mark. My first defence, once I'm confident with tide and sea conditions, is to get right down close to the layline. This means a port tack predator who tacks below me will struggle to lay, and if he tacks inside two boat lengths he will certainly break rule 18.3 as I will have to luff above close hauled.

"Despite this, I see Pink approaching as if to tack below. I bear away and aim 2 feet in front of her transom. She will probably deduce that I am not laying, take my transom, and join the queue behind. She might tack early and fail to lay the mark. At worst, she will tack in what looks like a lee bow position. I will then use the speed I have gained to climb back into clear wind, and, if she is lucky enough to lay the mark, give her a friendly wave as we bear off around her stationary bow at the windward mark." (see photos 8.5 to 8.10)

Photo 8.5 *GBR sees BEL, the port attacker*

Photo 8.6 *GBR bears away to close the gap*

Photo 8.7 *BEL is forced to tack early to avoid infringing*

Photo 8.8 *GBR now uses the speed he gained to sail high out of trouble*

Photo 8.9 *BEL is now unable to lay the mark*

Photo 8.10 *"See you later!"*

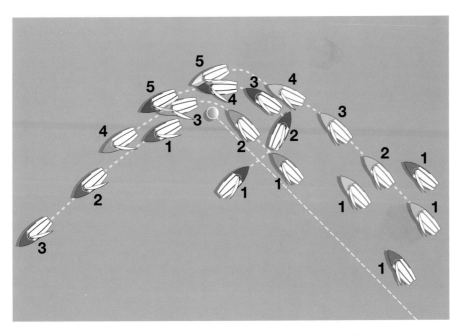

Fig 8.7 Mauve sails across Orange's bow, and tacks safely to windward

Keep your cool!

"It's all gone horribly wrong; we are approaching a congested windward mark on port tack! We are back in Mauve, and can just cross our old friend Orange. If we try to tack inside, we would certainly infringe. If we duck, we'll have to duck the lot, even Shocking Pink! We ignore the mark; keep going on port across Orange's bow. (He certainly doesn't want us to tack here!) Once clear, we can tack onto starboard in a space, and follow him round." (fig 8.7)

Control the leeward boat

"We're approaching the starboard layline, in Mauve, with Pink just below us. There is a fair amount of adverse tide on the mark, we really want Pink to sail well past the layline to leave room for us to round inside. In position 1 there is plenty of room for her to tack onto starboard and force us about. We take control, by bearing off hard to close the gap down to one boat width separation from Pink. Now she can't tack onto starboard without infringing. We have control, and can choose our layline." (fig 8.8)

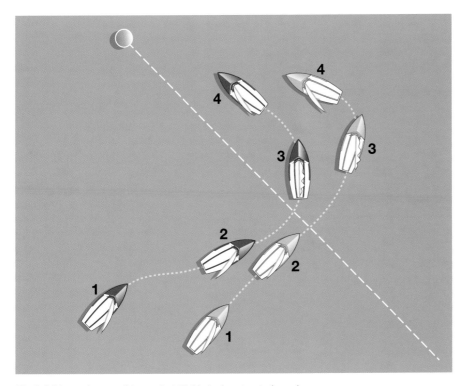

Fig 8.8 Mauve bears off to control Pink's tack onto starboard

Control the layline

Photo 8.11 ISR is on starboard tack, below the layline

Photo 8.12 As GER and NOR duck, ISR tacks to windward

Photo 8.13 ISR controls GER and NOR, and picks his layline

Photo 8.14 Only tacking once, ISR has reached a comfortable lay

Photo 8.15 ISR controls the fleet all the way to the mark

Photo 8.16 "Goodbye"

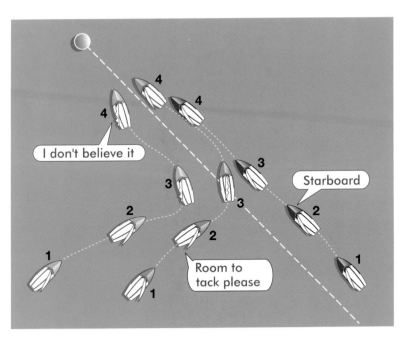

Fig 8.9 *Orange finds a starboard tacker to force Pink to tack early*

"Room to tack"

"The roles now reversed, we are in Orange. Pink is now trying to force us to the layline by bearing away to stop us tacking. We spot Mauve on the layline, and adjust our speed and direction so she is sure to force us about. Once we call room to tack, Pink is immediately obliged to tack or call "you tack" and keep clear. Nice move! (fig 8.9)

"However, if there is more than one boat to windward, this is definitely a high risk move. It will be virtually impossible to time the call so that they are all able to respond in time for us to keep clear of Mauve, and to lay the mark. That's because if Pink calls 'you tack', or tacks early, we're obliged to tack immediately."

Fig 8.10 *Orange slows to cause an overlap. Now he is entitled to room*

Force the overlap

"We are in Orange, along with our friend Pink. We have both found a huge advantage from the port side of the course. Pink is a little higher, and as things stand, will stop us from tacking around the mark. At two boat lengths, we slow down. Pink is not entitled to room. She has to bear off and becomes overlapped to leeward ...perfect! She now has to give us room to round the mark, including the tack!"

Which rules apply?

"This section is best read with rule book open!"

Rule 18: the mark rounding rule does not apply to beating boats on opposite tacks. Port tack gives way to starboard tack, and a boat tacking gives way to a boat that is on a tack (fig 8.11).

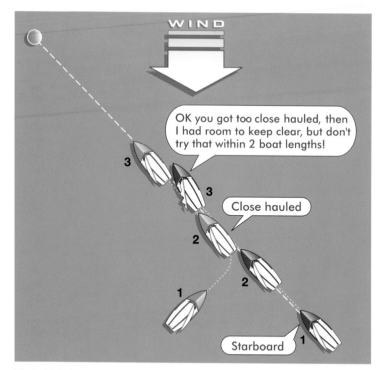

Fig 8.11 Rules 11 and 13 at the mark

Rule 18.3: opposite tack boats tacking within two boat lengths of the mark, further reduces the rights of a tacking boat. Not only does Pink have to keep clear while tacking, if Mauve has to sail above close hauled to keep clear, even after the tack is complete, Pink has fouled (fig 8.12).

Additionally, if Pink tacks inside two boat lengths and Mauve establishes an inside overlap, Pink has to give room. If Pink can't keep clear, she has fouled.

But, if Mauve has overstood, there is a subtle difference.

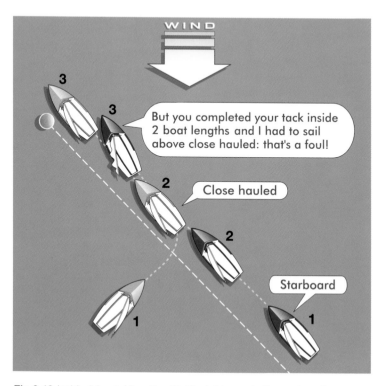

Fig 8.12 Inside 2 boats' lengths, Pink's rights are further reduced

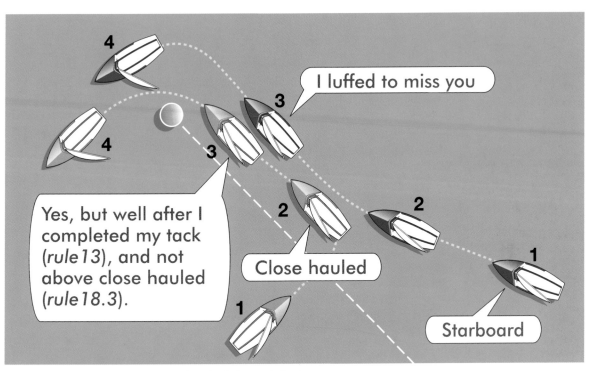

Fig 8.13 Mauve does not luff above close hauled: no rule broken

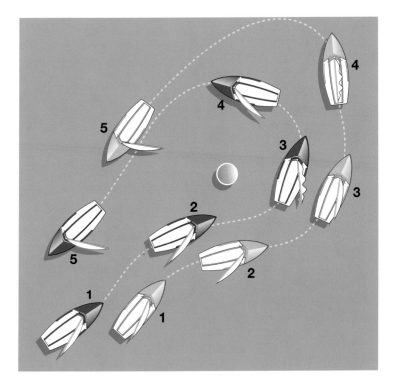

Fig 8.14 Mauve had an overlap when Pink reached two boat lengths: Pink has to give room

(fig 8.13) So long as Orange completes her tack before Mauve has to start keeping clear, she only fouls if Mauve has to luff above close hauled. Fig 8.6 p109 shows how Mauve can stop Orange pulling off this move.

Rule 18.2: If two boats on the same tack are rounding a mark, and an overlap was established before two boat lengths, the normal mark rounding rules apply: the inside boat is entitled to room to round the mark (fig 8.14).

Figure speech bubbles: "Shucks", "You are past head to wind: you have to keep clear! Go away!", "You are clear ahead! I have to keep clear"

Fig 8.15 *There was no overlap when Pink reached two boats' lengths: - as soon as she passes head to wind she must keep clear of Orange*

However, if there is no overlap, as soon as Pink passes head to wind, she loses her rights under rule 18.3,c. Unless Pink can complete her tack onto starboard and subsequently Orange has room to keep clear, she'll have to wait for Orange to round first (fig 8.15). (There is a solution for Pink: see fig 8.10 page 113.)

Rule 19:

Room to tack at an obstruction, does apply. So a port tack boat can ask a windward port tack boat for room to tack to avoid a starboard boat. A boat to leeward can use the approaching pack to manipulate boats to windward, so long as he times his call right (see fig 8.9 page 113).

When it all goes wrong….

The windward mark gives plenty of opportunities to start the recovery from a bad beat. If there is lots of tide on the mark, we've got plenty of time to see how it is affecting the boats ahead, and allow for it.

Now is the time to apply any lessons to the rest of the race: "Where did it all go wrong? Are there any consequences for the next leg? (Will one side of the run be favoured, will the first reach now be tight/broad?) Where is the pressure? The boats ahead may be too busy defending to notice the bigger picture. In an asymmetric fleet, an early gybe or gybe-set into pressure and away from the luffing pack will often bring us right back into contention.

Don't relax!
The temptation, near the end of a long hard slog upwind, is to relax and look forward to the offwind leg. But after the start, the windward mark is the next most congested part of the course. A two boat lengths gain could be equivalent to tens of places!

"My basic rules for windward mark tactics are:
- *Ensure that other boats are not in a position to prevent us from executing our strategy: don't let a pack of boats round inside and prevent a gybe set, if that was the plan.*
- *Stay in phase with the wind shifts for as long as possible.*
- *Find a 'lane' allowing a minimum time in dirty wind.*
- *Keep out of trouble: avoid incidents and bale out of vulnerable situations early: avoid a high risk port tack approach in closely congested fleets.*
- *Do not allow port tackers an opportunity to round inside.*
- *Keep the pressure on, think ahead, remember what your objectives for the next leg are, and get stuck in!"*

The reaching legs

A reach is a leg which can be comfortably laid on one gybe. In this chapter we'll look at reaching strategy, and tactical opportunities, for any offwind leg which will definitely not require a gybe to fetch the mark. A spacer leg, though short, falls within this definition. An offwind leg which may require a gybe can be regarded as a run for technical purposes: see chapter 10.

"We are at the 420 world championships at Hayling Island, UK. Our top ranked men's team gets everything right on the first beat. A left hand shift before the start gave the beat some 20 degrees of skew, making it a heavily port biased beat. Our team started near the starboard end, enabling them to quickly make a move onto the longer port tack. Making the most of the small oscillations, they comfortably lead the bunch on the right of the course.

"Many of the front runners started near the 'favoured' pin end, but were forced out towards the port layline by boats to windward; they are now close to the port layline so unable to make any use of the shifts. Our team lead round the windward mark, and execute a faultless slick hoist. The reaching mark is on their bow: it's a broad reaching leg assisted by some classic Hayling bay waves. No one can catch them now!

"The chasing bunch don't hoist immediately: they are suspicious that the leg seems too broad. At last one of the middle runners spots the real reaching mark: the 20 degree shift has turned the leg into a 2 sail reach, and our top team is headed for the outside leeward mark! By the time they realise, it's too late! They disconsolately drop the kite, beating back to round the reaching mark with the tail enders!"

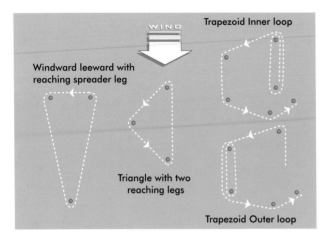

Fig 9.1 *Four classic course configurations which include at least one reaching leg*

Fig 9.2 *The mark always appears to windward of the bow, especially from the trapeze*

As we hinted in chapter 8 the tactics for the reach begin well before the rounding mark. Our pre-start routine should already have given some idea of how tight the reach is likely to be, whether it's an easy spinnaker leg, or a marginal call. If the 420 team in Ryan's story had thought about the impact of a left hand shift, they would have expected a tight 2 sail reach to the reaching mark.

As with the beat, we'll first look at the reach as a race against time, with no other boats to contend with, then look at offensive and defensive tactics to stick as close as possible to this "racing line".

Reaching strategy: the race against the clock.
"Imagine a time trial, with no other boats on the course. With no distractions, we can easily form a set of rules which will define the fastest route down the reaching leg."

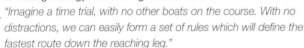

Sail the shortest course

The photo (9.1) shows the 420 fleet's classic reaching "great circle route". All other things being equal, the shortest course between two points is the straight line route. However, when steering from the windward side of the boat, the reaching mark always looks to windward of the bow.

When sailing the outer loop of a trapezoid course, (fig 9.1) the fleet is generally close packed after the first beat. We therefore treat the first part of the reach exactly as for a triangular course. However, when sailing the inner loop, the fleet is always more spread out after the extra windward leeward legs. In this case, an early hoist is far less likely to precipitate a mass of boats rolling through to windward. On the outer loop reach, a quick set and sailing the rhumb line gives the best chance of gaining an overlap on the boats ahead.

Photo 9.1 *The classic great circle route. Look just how far to windward of the rhumb line the fleet is dragged. Yet once the spinnakers are hoisted, it's an easy lay*

Even with no other boats to suck the fleet to windward, most helmsmen will naturally sail a "great circle route" to windward of the rhumb line, and lose time against the clock (fig 9.2). The simplest way to practice sailing the rhumb line is by picking up a transit on a piece of land behind the mark. If the land moves left against the mark, steer further right, and vice versa. The transit also aids sailing down the rhumb line in a cross tide situation, where the tide or current can gently sweep the boat away from the racing line, forcing a final approach to the reaching mark directly against the tide, while the "rhumb liners" sail straight by (fig 9.3).

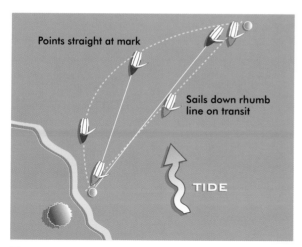

Fig 9.3 *Orange keeps the tree lined up with the mark, and sails the straight line course*

Sail fast

"That's easy to say, but we often get to the windward mark in good shape, then relax and fall back into the pack. There can be bigger differences in boat speed offwind than upwind. It may be difficult to turn a speed advantage into a major place gain, but it's certainly no trouble to turn a lapse of concentration into a loss."

Sail in maximum breeze

In patchy conditions, wind strength will always be the most fundamental natural asset. Sailing high to get into a band of pressure, or low to stay in it for longer, will ensure the higher average hull speed more than compensates for a little extra distance sailed. The old maxim "sail high in the lulls, low in the gusts" is a good one in conditions of varying strength.

"Sailing high in the lulls gets us up into the next band of breeze earlier. Sailing low in the puffs keeps us in the pressure for longer, and keeps us tracking towards the mark."

The highs and lows should be around a mean of the rhumb line course to the mark. We are simply using the gusts to improve our overall v.m.g. toward the mark. This technique also applies when it is the apparent wind strength that is changing, for example when big waves are providing surfing conditions. Once the boat is surfing on a wave, we use the apparent wind increase and header to make ground to leeward.

Look out for persistent change

If the wind is persistently moving in one direction, or either increasing or decreasing through the whole period of the leg, the straight line may not be the fastest option. If the wind is persistently heading, it's likely to pay to sail higher and faster above the layline. As the wind continues to head and we proceed along the leg, the "hot" angle will eventually take us straight to the mark.

If it's persistently lifting, it may pay to sail below the rhumb line to prevent the final approach to the reaching mark in the headed wind being broad and slow.

If the wind is steadily dropping in strength, it is likely to pay to initially head well below the rhumb line, making good ground to leeward in the greatest pressure, and staying with the stronger breeze for as long as possible. This will enable a hotter angle in the lighter breeze later on in the leg. Conversely, if there is persistently increasing pressure, sailing high of the rhumb line will mean the stronger wind comes earlier, giving more wind so more speed for the whole leg.

A persistent change in the tide may also overrule the straight line rule. For example, if the tide in fig 9.3 is strengthening in time, or in position as the leg develops, a course sailed below the rhumb line would give the fastest sailing angle for the longest time period. Simply sailing the rhumb line results in sailing a slower and slower angle as the tide increases. We would have to sail a broader and broader angle to stay on course.

Hoist or hold?

"In a hypothetical drag race, my general rule would be: if it's marginal, hoist the kite. My reason: if the kite can be *flown for part of the leg, it will pay to sail a longer course to achieve this. It's really hard to judge how far and how high to two sail down a marginal reach before hoisting, but it's easy to know when to drop it to give a nice fast two-sailer to the reaching mark. How many times have you two-sailed with the pack to half way down the reaching leg, then hoisted to find the rest of the leg is an easy lay? However, real life can be very different to drag racing: on a tight reach there is a real danger that a boat immediately behind will roll us during the hoist, to be followed by most of the fleet. Fleet tactics may have to override optimum strategy!"*

Set up for the next leg

From half way (less on a short leg) down a reaching leg, the exact "racing line" will be affected by the type and rounding direction of the next leg. If the next leg is a run, there may be a favoured side: if an early gybe is indicated an approach from a high angle may enable the boat and crew to set up. However, as with the windward mark, failing to defend an inside overlap may wreck this plan. If the reach was too tight for the kite, it may be worth sailing high to get it set just before, rather than just after the reaching mark. This technique is particularly useful in conditions where a standard hoist followed by a gybe with the kite set is so much easier than a white knuckle two sail gybe followed by a windward hoist.

If the next leg is a beat, it is vital that the mark approach allows for a controlled drop and smooth rounding.

Now add boats

"The next task is to try to apply these rules in the context of a competitive and uncooperative fleet, which is intent on turning our cosy drag race into an obstacle course."

We'll look at a number of typical courses and situations, and work through the tactical options for each one.

The spreader leg

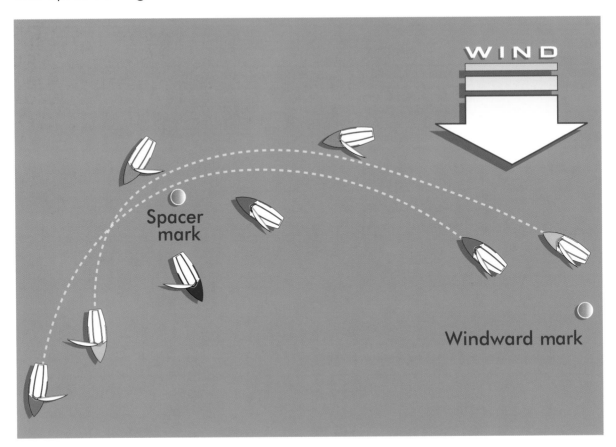

Fig 9.4 The spreader leg

Photo 9.2 *The spreader leg presents few opportunities for gains, but many for losses*

Asymmetric classes love throwing this little tactical dilemma into their windward-leeward courses. Perfectly laid, it is too tight to spinnaker but an easy fetch with two sails. It is simply a safety mark to prevent unsighted running boats "t-boning" port tack layliners. Its effect is to spread the fleet out as everyone defends from behind, allowing the boats ahead to roll away (photo 9.2). But a small shift, or a skewed spacer leg, gives several tactical possibilities.

Wind lifted on starboard

"A small starboard lift may make the spinnaker viable. However, hoisting immediately round the mark will only work if there is a good space behind. A boat close behind will climb with speed during the manoeuvre, and blanket the hoisting boat, preventing its spinnaker from filling. A 'roll' is inevitable, and it won't be just one boat. This is a high tariff tactic with a potential big loss. One option is to sail high and fast, clear of the pack until there is space to hoist and clear the boats to leeward. Once up and running in the 'fast lane', it is possible to continue to gain places.

"This tactic may initially gain places: but don't lose sight of where we want to be on the run! The leg is so short that we need to think back from the spreader mark. Sailing high and hoisting may work if it's simply a badly laid course. But if we

know that the wind has lifted on starboard, we also know that it has headed on port. This means that an early gybe is indicated on the run.

"If we are outside a pack of boats we have just failed to roll, we will have to wait for them to gybe. This may never happen! So we should only allow ourselves to become overlapped outside a group of boats if we are certain to break the overlap by the spreader mark. If we are not, it's better to stick to the bigger picture, concentrate on defending, and prepare for a slick hoist gybe or gybe hoist out to the left side of the course."

Wind headed on starboard

"Now the opposite is true. We want to sail the first part of the run on the starboard header. We simply must not get rolled, or round with a boat overlapped on the outside at the spacer mark, as an early gybe for clear wind will be a disaster. We'd be forced to take the short leg first on the run. Instead, we make our intentions clear. We sail high from the windward mark, force the boats behind to take our transom. We then concentrate on sailing as fast as possible to the point a boat length to windward of the spacer mark which is our cue to begin the hoist (photo 9.3). If we are overlapped outside other boats at the mark: no problem. A slick hoist will take us through them with speed."

Photo 9.3 *Barbarians has sailed high on the spreader leg, defending the windward side. They have gained just enough height to make a clean hoist before the spreader mark*

The traditional reach

For the leader of the race, or of for a bunch of boats with a reasonable space ahead, priorities on the reach have never been easier:

"Defend, hoist, extend. If there is a boat on your tail, defence requires simply an early indication that there is no way to pass to windward. A confident luff, a shake of the head, even a smile - whatever it takes to see the boat behind conceding, and pointing at or below our transom (fig 9.5). Once the spinnaker is up, natural forces will see the boats behind climbing higher and higher to defend/attack each other, while each gust takes the leaders closer to the rhumb line and further ahead, or closer to the next pack of boats ahead."

open for the leeward attack route, which occasionally opens up behind a big group of aggressive luffers intent on preventing each other from hoisting their kites."

Again, any defensive luff has to be firm, early, and clear. This should encourage most windward aggressors that the best way forward is as a parallel group rather than as "great circle routers".

A boat handling error during the hoist by a boat close ahead may provide an attacking opportunity. Even better, that one boat may be slowing a bunch.

"Watch for a faster boat which has gained an involuntary leeward overlap on a boat still hoisting: this may be a chance to roll them both. We try to hide our intentions as late as possible, but are always prepared to sail high and fast at exactly the moment the boat ahead is unable to respond. As soon as we are through to windward, we are straight back to speed mode, once again working the gusts to get down to the racing line."

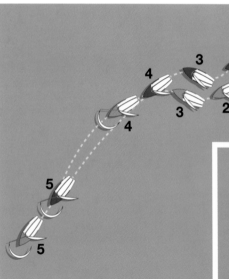

Fig 9.5 *Orange's sharp, confident luff makes it absolutely clear to Mauve that there is no way through to windward*

For those less fortunate, struggling around the windward mark in a pack of boats, the first priority is clear wind.

"While trying to develop a lane, we must not be dragged way to windward of the rhumb line, by boats which are so far back that they will not affect our wind. If back in the pack, we always keep an eye

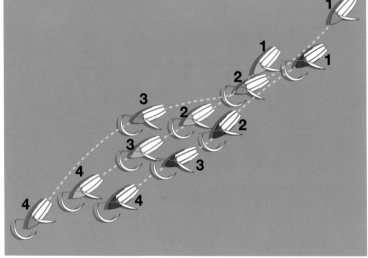

Fig 9.6 *Orange spots that Pink's slow hoist has caused Mauve to become trapped to leeward. He attacks to windward*

However, if it is clear that the boats ahead have good boat handling and reasonable speed, attacking options are limited.

"In this case we point at or just below the boat ahead's transom, to encourage him to sail the rhumb line route, watch for a mistake, and work hard at trying to establish an overlap before the gybe mark".

Leeward attack route

"This only works when there is a bunch ahead sailing high, and a reasonable gap behind. The key is to get the kite up early and focus on using any increase in pressure to get immediate leeward separation from the pack. We keep sailing as far below the rhumb line as we dare without slowing the boat, and only luff to point at the gybe mark when we can sail straight to it at a fast reaching angle (fig 9.7). With luck, we will now be able to see clear wind from in front of the pack, who are now reaching down to the mark at slow broad angles, and even if not clear ahead we'll have an inside overlap for a windward exit from the gybe mark."

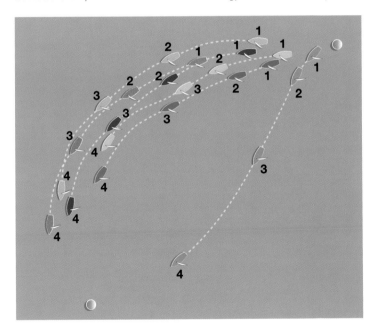

***Fig 9.7** The pack sail each other high. Orange rounds with a gap behind, and utilises a gust to sail down onto a clear leeward attack route*

Triangle, tight first reach

"Let's assume a reach which is definitely kite-able, but possibly too close to be sure to carry the spinnaker for the whole leg. At the head of a pack, the traditional conservative approach is a two-sail reach until the first boat behind hoists. I've already talked about the optimum 'drag race' route, and have seen world champions and silver medallists turn a small lead into an invincible one by hoisting immediately, and maximising the gain. If marginal, we can gain the last 10 boat lengths to leeward with pole still set but spinnaker halyard dumped. To make the early hoist work, the gap behind has to be sufficient that we can complete the hoist and be up to speed before the boat behind attacks. Our commitment has to be absolute: a firm bear away to provide a stable platform for the crew, with spinnaker guy and pole lift cleated right on the marks for a quick getaway.

"If back in the pack, a hoist on the mark while surrounded by boats is unlikely to be successful: once one two-sail reaching boat comes over the top you'll be in the slow lane for some time! Work clear to get clear wind a couple of boat lengths above the 'slow lane', hoist as soon as the boats behind put their bow down, but don't get sucked into the great circle route by boats who are never going to fly their kites! The leeward attack route on a shy reach is not really an option unless you fancy a beat back from the leeward mark!"

Second reach

Two factors make tactics on the second reach subtly different from the first. The end of the second reach marks the start of the next beat. Boat on boat positioning becomes increasingly important, as an inside overlap and smooth rounding will frequently gain more places than were available on the whole leg.

A leeward attack on the second reach is only likely to work in exceptional circumstances (light wind or strong tidal influence). Not only will leeward attackers be outside at the mark, they would also have to break the overlap to pass a boat to windward: this requires gaining yet another boat length's distance. In contrast, on the first reach an overlap was all that was needed to lead around the next mark.

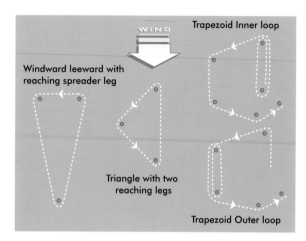

Fig 9.1 *Four classic course configurations which include at least one reaching leg*

The trapezoid reach

The first reach of both inner and outer loop trapezoid courses is followed by a run. As the reach progresses, positioning for the reaching mark and strategy for the run become increasingly important, just as on the spacer leg.

"From half way down the trapezoid reach we are thinking about the reaching mark approach, positioning ourselves against the other boats. Our objective is to get us in phase with the pressure and shifts, and clear of distractions, right at the start of the run." (photo 9.4)

Final reach: trapezoid

Ryan's view is that the final reach and fetch are only added to a trapezoid course to spread the fleet out, and make it easier to identify finishers' sail numbers. Although it's difficult to gain places on the final two legs, it is certainly possible to lose places by relaxing early. So save the refreshments until after the finish. Tactically, there is rarely an opportunity to pass to leeward. It is absolutely vital to protect the windward side of the reach, and to maintain the inside berth before the fetch to the finish. Whichever end of the line is favoured, it is rarely possible to reach it first from the outside berth at the penultimate mark. The message is: defend, but be ready to take advantage of any competitors' mistakes.

No more tactics

"In general, the reaching legs give a much smaller range of strategic and tactical opportunity for gaining places. First class speed and trim techniques, through the full range of conditions, are absolutely vital if the reach is to be anything other than a defensive phase of the race. To anyone planning to gain places on the reach, I'd recommend one full day's on-the-water reaching practice for every hour of background reading! A little coaching may help, too!"

Photo 9.4 *The winning strategy for this final run is to gybe set into more pressure. A late windward attack on the reach could result in a delayed gybe*

The run

More and more regattas and championships are raced around windward leeward courses. Why is this? It's fun learning and applying the techniques required for fast reaching, and great blasting out to or from the race course on a toe clinging 3-sailer. However, the reach provides limited tactical opportunities or challenges. In a big championship, the first close reach might offer a couple of boats the chance to make large gains and recover from a bad start, but for most of the fleet the reaches are largely defensive affairs, the rich getting richer. Ryan is a passionate supporter of windward leeward courses:

"The run is a natural extension of the beat. It's harder to defend, because the boats behind can blanket those ahead. New breeze comes from behind, giving plenty of opportunities to close the gap. Choosing whether to sail high for speed, or soak to sail less distance, adds another dimension to downwind sailing."

Strategy on the run
"We used the time available before the start to check out the conditions, and form a strategy for the first beat. The beat should have confirmed or corrected these predictions, so gives us a chance to make a similar plan for the run. Here are some of the factors I consider when forming my run strategy."

Pressure rules!
"Except when it's really light or heavy, the angle we steer to the wind on the beat stays pretty constant through the wind range. Therefore upwind, the biggest gains are usually made through taking advantage of wind shifts to sail the shortest course. Priorities downwind are usually reversed: a few knots change in wind speed means we go faster, or can sail a much deeper angle. Sailing in more pressure is generally more important than sailing to the shifts."

Two factors magnify this effect:

 "Clearly, when we are beating, we are travelling in the opposite direction to the wind. That means that the gusts travel down the course towards us, have their effect, then continue down the course and away. When running, we are both going in the same direction. The gust stays with us for longer, and the advantage of sailing in the pressure is multiplied. In fact, by working hard on technique it's possible to carry one gust all the way down the run."

Because a run takes the boat away from, not into, the new wind, the time period of the oscillating shifts is greatly increased. If we sail upwind at 5 knots, in 10 knots breeze, the shift patterns pass us at 10 + 5 = 15 knots. If we are going downwind at 5 knots, they come past at 10 − 5 = 5 knots: that means the shift period will be three times longer. An oscillating shift pattern upwind can become a persistent one downwind. There may not be time to consolidate a gain from a windshift by gybing across the fleet, as we would on the beat.

Windshifts

Having made these points, if the pressure is constant, there are gains to be made through getting the shifts right offwind. On the run, sailing in the headers gives the shortest distance to the mark.

Oscillating shifts

"For oscillating shifts, my rule of thumb on the final approach to the windward mark is: if we are headed; bear away and set to stay in the header. If we are lifted, gybe as soon as possible to get onto the headed tack." (figs 10.1 and 10.2)

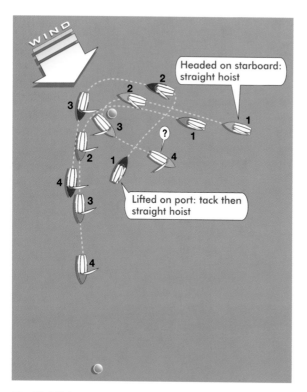

Fig 10.1 *If the oscillation is left of mean, starboard will be the favoured gybe*

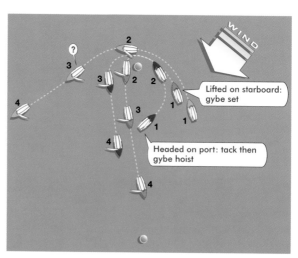

Fig 10.2 *If the oscillation is right of mean, port will be the favoured gybe*

Wind bend

For a wind bend, the shortest route down the run will be to follow the fast track up the beat: sailing towards the centre of the bend. This means tending to the same side of the run as paid on the beat, i.e. we aim to sail back down the wake we made on the beat. In fig 10.3 Orange sails two thirds the distance of Pink by sailing to the inside of the bend.

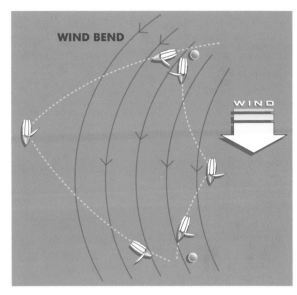

Fig 10.3 *Winning strategy: sail to the inside of the bend*

Tidal effects

In general, if one side of the beat has paid due to tide, the opposite will pay on the run. It's fairly easy to work this out if the tide is roughly in line with (favourable or otherwise) the leg.

If the tide is skewed across the course, it's much harder to judge the layline to the leeward mark. Effectively, the tide makes one gybe longer than the other.

 "Don't forget: the race officer may have compensated for the tide and set a true beat, the run may be skewed; it may even be a one tack leg."

Orange takes the safest option, sailing the long leg first making the layline easier to judge, and reducing the chance of being swept past the mark (fig 10.4). Mauve has to judge a long cross-tide layline, and overstands, having to sail a hot angle to lay the mark, wasting time and distance.

If the tidal strength or direction is changing during the run, the situation becomes more complex. It may be possible to figure out the fastest route using tidal stream atlases, but in small boat racing the only realistic solution is "watch and learn!"

"My golden rule is, try to plan a route which gives the most favourable current when it's strongest, least favourable when it's weakest."

Long leg first

As with the beat, sailing the long leg first makes judging the layline easier, maximises opportunities to gain from unpredicted wind shifts, and minimises risk.

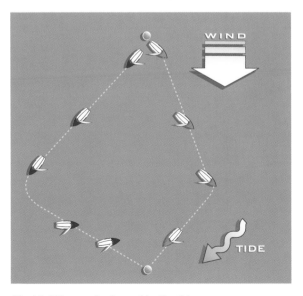

Fig 10.4 *The run is skewed by the tide*

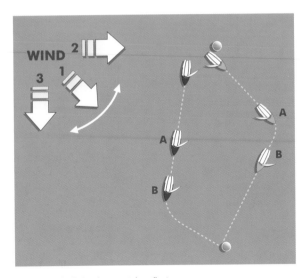

Fig 10.5 *Sail the longest leg first*

Mauve has chosen starboard gybe, which takes her closer towards the leeward mark. Pink has gybed onto port. At point A, Pink has to judge her layline, even though she is still closer to the windward mark then the leeward mark. This is difficult enough in steady conditions. At point B both boats are the same sailing distance from the leeward mark, with Mauve approaching her much less critical layline. If the wind shifts to 2, Mauve will lay the mark without gybing, but pink will have further to sail to the mark, and may have to drop her kite. If the wind shifts to 3, Mauve can gybe early, and has a short port leg to the mark, while Pink has a very broad run of twice the distance.

Sort the priorities

"As with the beat, I split the run into sectors, each part having its own (sometimes conflicting) priorities. The beat will have given us a pretty good indication of which are the most important natural assets of the day, these define our strategy. Fig 10.6 shows how this strategy fits in around the other priorities".

Clear wind

On a beat, sailing in dirty wind simply lets the leaders get further ahead. On the run, it lets boats behind come past. The first priority on rounding is to keep clear wind. If we are planning to go right, this may need a quick luff to send a clear message to the boats behind. If the bunch behind is a big aggressive one, an early soak in the first gust may leave them luffing out of reach of our air. If neither tactic works, the only solution is a couple of gybes into a clear lane.

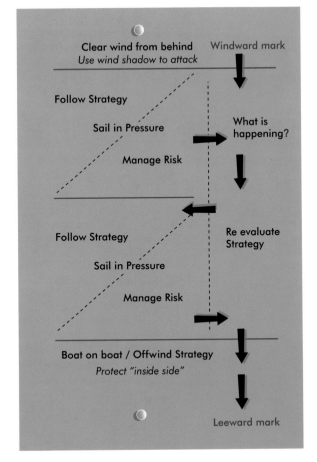

Fig 10.6

"Gybe in maximum pressure, anticipating rather than reacting to an attacker's wind shadow. In most boats, a gybe in a gust loses little distance, and if it results in sailing back towards the centre of the gust it may even produce a gain."

If planning to gybe at the windward mark, it's important to carefully watch the boats immediately behind (photo 10.1). If possible, we keep them overlapped outside so we can gybe first. If that's not possible, and the boats behind look set up to gybe at the same time, we can either sail high and fast on the new gybe to reach clear wind, or delay the gybe until we can see a lane forming.

The disadvantage of sailing high is that we end up on the outside of the course compared with the boats behind, which means they can gybe on top of us when we come back (photo 10.4 p131). If the gusts and lulls allow, the controlling move is to keep clear wind inside the fleet, giving plenty of opportunity to attack boats ahead as they, in turn, gybe back to the centre of the course.

Follow strategy

"Once in clear wind, with freedom to follow the plan, we can really start working on the big picture. We keep watching for the gusts coming down the course, and try to use each one to squeeze us nearer to the favoured side of the course."

Photo 10.1 *GRE opted for a straight set. SUI has gybe-set into a great gap. GBR delayed the gybe by an instant, giving ITA the opportunity to attack*

Leverage and risk

We have discussed leverage and risk on the beat. Exactly the same principles apply on the run. The more separated we are from the fleet sideways, the bigger the effect of any windshift and the more likely we are to find more or less wind. Big separation leads to big gains or losses.

"Once again, working out the paying side and banging the corners may be fun, but it's not a formula for consistent success. Most regattas are won through steady accumulation, this means matching the risks to the situation, and balancing strategic moves with more immediate requirements."

Upwind, the gains made due to a shift are "banked" by tacking across between the wind and the fleet. The same principle applies on the run: to consolidate a gain through a header, gybe back across the pack (photo 10.2).

Photo 10.2 *07 has gybed into a perfect position to cover the fleet*

When positioned to leeward of the pack, exposure can be reduced by sailing higher and faster, reducing separation. This would be the consolidating move if the fleet was behind and to windward, with more wind on their side.

Have we got it right?

"If not, at some stage we may need to cut our losses. Nothing is certain in sailing, so we keep checking that our predictions are correct, that our strategy is working. If boats doing the opposite seem to be making gains, take the time to understand why, before reaching across to the other side of the course for that elusive 20 degree lift!"

Leeward mark positioning

On a really short running leg, there may not be time to pass boats through superior speed, boat handling, or strategy. In this case the jostling for the inside berth at the leeward mark begins as the running leg starts: the first boat to execute a fast gybe in clear wind controls the "inside side". They will be on starboard tack on the approach to the leeward mark, and if it's a port hand mark have an inside overlap as well! On a full size course, the patterns of boats begin to take shape with one third of the running leg left.

"We look at the positions of the boats across the leg, working back from the leeward mark to find a route which will give us clear wind, no-one overlapped inside, and where possible, an inside overlap on the boats in the pack ahead. It is never too early to start working towards this aim." (photo 10.3)

Alternatively the "round the outside" tactic can work in light wind particularly when there is a lot of adverse tide. In this situation the "herding instinct" often causes a bunch of boats to gybe too early to sail fast towards the buoy. The bunch slows itself down, sailing deeper and deeper, making little progress on the mark. Once the spinnakers start coming down the situation gets worse. It's possible that a fast moving boat approaching on a hot port gybe, to leeward of the pack, with a late drop and neat rounding, can be around and on the next leg while the shouting still continues! More on this in chapter 13.

Boat on boat
How do we spot the shifts downwind?

"It's tricky. The problem is that a small pressure change gives a bigger angle change than a significant shift, so the compass on its own does not help. It is definitely a lift if the kite sheet can be eased as a gust hits, with no change of direction. However in a lull, the boat does not instantly slow down. The apparent wind moves forward, at the same time as the helm feels he needs to luff up. It may feel like a header, but it probably is not. Practice and communication between trimmer and helmsman are the keys to sniffing the shifts downwind."

When to gybe
"Stay in the gusts. In my boat we nominate someone in our boat to look upwind for pressure, for general trends, as well as local gusts. We stay in the gusts by gybing at maximum pressure; sailing back into a spreading gust rather than waiting until it begins to fade. We always look for an increase in pressure before making a tactical gybe."

Offensive gybe: *"We attack a boat ahead on the same gybe, by aiming for their leeward quarter. We gybe as they do, and exit with them perfectly positioned in our wind shadow." (photos 10.4, 5 and 6)*

Photo 10.3 *On a short leg, there may be no time for other factors to make a significant difference. Controlling the inside side may be the biggest priority*

Photo 10.4 *Yellow kite has soaked to a perfect position from which to attack Blue's gybe*

Photo 10.5 *Yellow shadows Blue's gybe*

Photo 10.6 *Despite a poor gybe, Yellow can use her wind shadow to gain an inside overlap on Blue*

The execution is the same for symmetric and asymmetric boats, but the offensive gybe has to be earlier with an asymmetric so we exit the gybe far enough forward to slow the other boat (fig 10.7). That means closely watching the boat ahead.

Fig 10.7 *The offensive gybe*

Mauve's only defence is to gybe as soon as he sees Orange making his move to leeward, or to bear away and stay parallel. But Mauve is not permitted to sail below his proper course unless he gybes. (ISAF rule 17.2)

Defensive gybe: The "safe leeward" position is the position ahead and to leeward, free of wind shadow from the windward boat or group of boats. It's position varies depending on the spinnaker configuration and boat speeds. To be confident of close manoeuvring downwind we need to know exactly where the edge of the wind shadow lies.

"The burgee gives a pretty good clue!"

"When gybing to defend from boats behind, we always gybe to leeward of their line, rather than on or to windward of it. For a good 'cover', start the gybe just as the opposition's line is crossed, to end up ahead and a small distance to leeward, clear of their wind shadow. This maintains tactical freedom (it's not possible for the other boat to gybe on our wind if we gybe again), and gives them an unfavourable quarter wave." (fig 10.7)

Photo 10.7 *The "safe leeward" position is further forward when apparent wind sailing. 088 is under no threat from 092, who is also too high to be able to attack when 088 gybes*

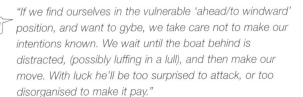

"If we find ourselves in the vulnerable 'ahead/to windward' position, and want to gybe, we take care not to make our intentions known. We wait until the boat behind is distracted, (possibly luffing in a lull), and then make our move. With luck he'll be too surprised to attack, or too disorganised to make it pay."

Sail them to the layline!

Once at the layline, there is often no opportunity for a boat ahead to gybe for clear wind (fig 10.8). Orange holds Mauve out until past Mauve's layline. Orange dictates the gybe point. Now Mauve is in bad air, with nowhere to go. Because it's now a straight line to the leeward mark, he has no opportunity to return the favour either.

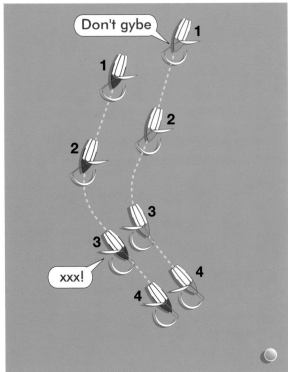

Fig 10.8 *Orange is clear astern and can force Mauve to a reaching layline, slowing Mauve out of the gybe and gaining an easy overlap*

Crossing transoms

As the run progresses and the fleet begins to converge towards the leeward mark, clear lanes across to the inside track on port gybe are hard to find. By thinking ahead, it is possible to use a starboard tacker to clear a lane. This tactic works particularly well in asymmetric boats.

Fig 10.9 Mauve "ducks" by bearing off, slowing enough to create a clear lane on his left hand side

Rather than luffing and accelerating around Orange's transom and into Green's wind shadow, Mauve bears away and slows down early. Once Orange has sailed past, Mauve accelerates into the space he has created (fig 10.9).

Sailing fast downhill

Specific downwind techniques vary enormously through the range of racing craft. Every class or type has its own characteristic and mode of sailing:

"Sailors who are fast downwind, quickly adapt their feel to a completely different style of boat. This includes boats with instruments and target figures, boats without, asymmetric and apparent wind driven machines, keelboats, and dinghies without spinnakers."

"The common themes to success are: learn from the class 'experts', develop lines of understanding and communication between trimmers and helmsman, and practise against similar craft."

Sailing the angles

As well as changing downwind techniques for different conditions, the ability to shift sailing modes downwind opens up tactical opportunities, in all configurations of sailboats.

"We must know the optimum angle and sailing techniques for our boat in every condition. Be prepared to switch between the three modes of downwind sailing: soaking, surfing, or blasting, when tactics dictate".

Soaking

Photo 10.8 Soaking mode

"We are simply aiming to sail the boat as close as possible in the direction of the leeward mark, without the spinnaker collapsing: a collapse of the spinnaker involves a large course alteration a long speed build". (photo 10.8)

Surfing

There is not enough power to plane permanently, to generate significant apparent wind, or overtake the waves.

The boat is sailed very much as for soaking mode.

"As well as acting on pressure calls from the crew, the helm works the boat and pumps the main to encourage the boat to surf down the waves, maximising time spent sailing downhill, using the speed generated to head closer to the mark." (photo 10.9)

Photo 10.9 *Surfing mode*

Apparent wind sailing

"This is what we sail for. Crew are now hiking/trapezing hard, the higher we sail, the more the apparent wind, the faster the boat goes. The boat just goes lower and faster. Forget surfing down the waves… we are just trying to avoid them!"

The more extreme the boat and conditions the bigger obstacles the waves appear! To prevent a catastrophic nosedive, the crew are ready to rag the spinnaker to slow the boat down.

In these conditions a small wind increase creates a big change in sailing angle. This means that in variable conditions it's very easy to overstand the leeward mark.

"Apparent wind sailing is not limited to asymmetric boats, I have seen Fireball and 505 championship races won by crews trapezing down the run… so next time the club racing is abandoned get out there, get training, and have some fun!"

After a hard windward leg it's tempting to set the kite, get the drinks out, and relax down the run. But the fact that the gusts are coming from behind gives us a real chance to make significant gains. Even if we pass no boats, the run gives a great opportunity to arrive at the leeward mark in a position to attack the bunch ahead.

Photo 10.10 *Apparent wind sailing*

The leeward mark

A bad leeward mark approach and rounding can undo all the good work done on the run, and severely limit opportunities at the start of the beat. A good approach can turn a marginal gain into an overlap, and a good rounding creates the opportunity for clear wind and the freedom to tack or carry on as strategy dictates.

"Approaching the leeward mark in our 1720 sportsboat, we have caught a gaggle of slower (but bigger) boats from the start ahead. Four boat lengths from the mark, it's clear that we won't make the overlap in time. 'No worries: early drop.' We turn the boat downwind, slowing and making room for a nice smooth rounding. The boats ahead are all overlapped. The boat inside has started his turn too close to the mark: there is obviously going to be a space between him and the mark on the exit. All we need to do is to luff across his transom and we'll exit to windward of the group with speed. Now the turn begins: a little leeward heel to unload the rudder, and the boat accelerates as the sails are sheeted on in time with the turn. Our bow starts to pass across his transom, about a foot clear. The crew smile smugly to each other with the satisfaction of a job well done.

"Is the pole in?"

"'Bang!' the shotgun sound of 6mm wall carbon snapping, as the outside boat starts to luff with our partly extended gennaker pole neatly threaded through his pushpit. 'We won't be so fast on the next run, then'."

The racing line

Unlike the start or the windward mark, there is rarely any strategic debate about how to exit the leeward mark. The best exit from a port hand leeward mark is almost invariably at full speed, next to the mark, on port tack. The helm should be able to reach out and touch the mark as we go by in full close hauled trim (photo 11.1). This leaves all strategic options open, and gives the best chance for clear air on the beat. We'll look at the exceptions to this basic rule later.

Imagine sailing a race against the clock with no other boats on the course. The slowest leg is usually the beat, because reaching boats go faster than beating boats, and beating boats can't sail straight towards the windward mark.

It therefore makes sense to minimise the upwind distance sailed. For this reason, even if there are no other boats, it will pay to execute the turn so it is done on the offwind leg, not the upwind. A smooth turn takes the least amount of speed off the boat. Orange's wide approach automatically leads to a tight exit (fig 11.1).

Pink aims at the leeward mark straight from her final gybe. She starts her gybe as she gets to the mark, and spends the first thirty seconds of the beat performing her turn, still sailing away from the windward mark. She loses a place, and the initiative.

Orange's rounding (fig 11.1, photo 11.1 p136/137) gives the best chance of sailing out of the leebow of the boats ahead, while slowing the boats behind, and leaves him free to tack at will. The smooth turn means that the boat is still faster than beating speed as it passes the mark. If there is a leeward boat overlapped outside, he may have to compromise the ultra wide approach a little. The leeward boat only has to allow room to round the mark, nothing more. (In practice the outside boat is usually so busy trying to create room for his own smooth rounding, that it is possible for Orange to stick pretty close to the racing line).

The challenging part of the leeward mark rounding is sorting just how to approach the mark with respect to the other boats to enable this perfect start to the next beat, and how to handle the boat to achieve it while minimising drag.

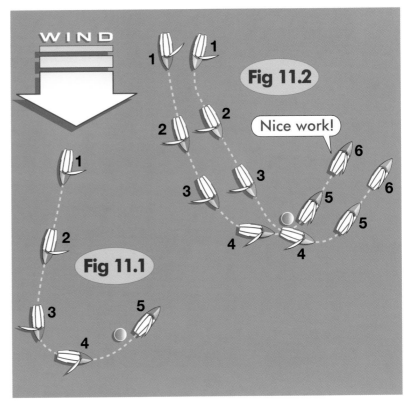

Fig 11.1 The racing line
Fig 11.2 Orange makes room, and luffs across Pink's transom

"The actual radius of the turn depends on the type of boat, and the prevailing conditions. Spend a day practising rounding a mark, preferably with a "buddy", to develop an appreciation of your boat's characteristics."

Add in some other competitors and Pink's roundings become even more disastrous. By exiting below the port layline from the mark, she is already in the dirty wind of boats ahead who have made good roundings. Being below the layline also makes tacking out of this "slow lane" difficult: it's unlikely that she would be able to complete a tack onto starboard without fouling boats which have made tight roundings just behind.

Photo 11.1 *Joe Fly's racing line gives them a tight exit with speed. They have gained almost a boat length's windward distance on the boat ahead*

The racing line

Photo 11.2 At a crowded leeward mark, ISR drops early, clearing a space ahead

Photo 11.3 ISR gybes two boat lengths abeam of the mark, leaving space for a smooth turn and tight exit

Photo 11.4 ISR is moving faster then normal beating speed

Photo 11.5 *They are close hauled at max speed as they pass the mark*

Photo 11.6 *Compare the result of ISR's rounding with the boats ahead and behind*

Around the outside

The outside route may work in some specific circumstances, so long as we are happy to commit to sailing on port towards the right hand side of the course for some time:

- Very light winds: A boat ahead which has slowed to clear an inside overlap may take a long time to accelerate. If there is a long line of boats all overlapped, the wait until they have all gone past may just be too long.
- Very strong winds: If the boat ahead is struggling to make the transition (main slow coming in, vang, outhaul/Cunningham/centreboard not set up/crew still dousing kite), we can simply put the bow down and plane through to leeward.

"Be aware of the pattern of the boats which have already rounded. If there is a nice gap ahead, the wide rounding might succeed. But if boats have made a tight rounding and are just ahead on port tack, we'll harden up straight into their wind shadow, with limited opportunities for escape."

What's the plan?

Well before the approach to the mark, we should have built a strategy for the beat, and even the next offwind leg. The offwind leg may dictate or favour a particular leeward mark approach: if the next off wind leg is a tight starboard reach we really want to drop the kite on the port side, and stow the pole on the starboard. The beat strategy is formulated in exactly the same way as the first beat, with the added benefit of lessons learnt on the first beat.

If there has been a large windshift, or the course is particularly badly laid, the beat will be predominantly one tack. The advantage will invariably be with the boats which get onto the long tack first, in a clear lane. In this case choosing a leeward mark strategy which gives this opportunity is the highest priority; more important than a couple of metres gain, or a last minute overlap.

"Start planning the exit before the mark approach. Most of the opposition will just take the leeward mark as it comes. This is our opportunity to start the next beat going the way we want, in clear wind."

If the left hand of the beat is favoured, the "around the outside" leeward mark rounding is definitely not appropriate. If the crew knows that we are looking for an early tack, we can be sure that the sheets are clear, the kite is packed, we are sitting out hard, and everyone is ready the moment the opportunity occurs. Ideally we do this while the boat ahead is still tidying up: if they tack first we may have to go beyond their line to find a clear lane. By putting our bow up every time their helmsman looks aft, we may persuade them that they don't have room to tack and clear.

Clear ahead

Mauve is under no pressure, and makes the ultimate smooth leeward mark rounding, gaining maximum upwind distance. He didn't wait until the last minute to set up for the rounding. As soon as he was confident that Pink couldn't establish an inside overlap in time, he dropped the spinnaker and began his preparation: he's in even more control if Pink ends up with a last minute outside overlap through not thinking ahead! If Pink is clear astern and Mauve wants to make her life even harder, he'll luff above close hauled as he passes the mark, forcing Pink to leeward and preventing any possibility of a "sail-on".

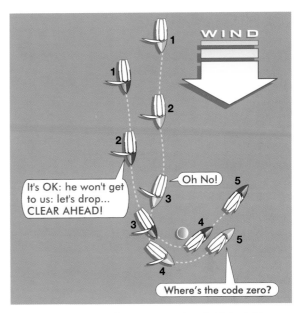

Fig 11.3 As soon as the status quo is established, Mauve begins preparing for the rounding

"The Wiggle"

The overlap began when the boats were more than two boats' lengths apart. Orange has worked out, ten boat lengths from the buoy, that he will not be able to break Mauve's overlap before two boat lengths. Orange simply luffs Mauve to the left side of the rhumb line. When he finally bears away and enters the two boat lengths circle, the line across Orange's transom is clear ahead of Mauve's bow, Mauve is not entitled to water.

Orange could have also used the wiggle if Mauve had gained the overlap from behind. However, if Orange had established the leeward overlap from behind, with the boats less than two boat lengths apart, this tactic would not work: Orange would not be allowed to sail above his proper course (Rule 17.1).

Fig 11.4 Orange luffs so the overlap is broken outside two boat lengths, when he bears away

Slower is faster

If Orange can't break the overlap through the wiggle, he has to slow the boat down by dropping early, over sheeting the mainsail, or pointing the boat dead downwind. This allows the inside boats to sail clear ahead and break the overlap. Orange then steers his racing line, luffs across the transoms of the boats ahead, and is in a perfect position to take advantage of any mistake. Even if the boats ahead round perfectly, Orange is free to tack or to sail high into clear wind. By sailing slowly he has reduced the length of his beat, and left all his options open. Rounding outside another boat or boats at a leeward mark generally leads to a greater distance to sail, dirty wind, and no escape route (photo 11.9).

 "But make sure the pole is retracted before luffing across the boat ahead's transom!"

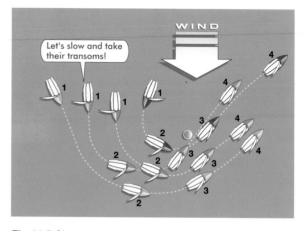

Fig 11.5 *Slower can be faster*

Buffalo girls

Sometimes the leeward mark is so congested that it's simply not possible to hit the perfect line, or to prevent an inside overlap. The classic scenario occurs with heavier boats, lightish winds, tide, and inside boats stuffing each other to a standstill. The "around the outside" tactic, though not guaranteed, can work in these situations.

 "We aim to approach the mark at a fast reaching angle with kite set. We are at maximum boat speed, directly to leeward of the bunch, at the apex of the turn. We keep sailing fast and free until through the dirt created by the traffic jam, and only then wind on the trim to achieve close hauled course. We sail low enough to keep our bow forward, and our sails just in clear wind (fig 11.6).

"As leeward boat,we are still right of way boat. So long as we give room, we can cramp the inside boat's rounding, forcing him into a tight speed killing turn, and exit with speed clear to leeward. If he's completely stopped (for example in foul tide) we may even be able to sail round his bow and still complete a tight rounding." (fig 11.7)

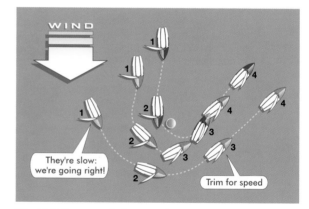

Fig 11.6 *Orange sails for speed and achieves a safe leeward position*

Fig 11.7 *The inside boats are moving so slowly that Orange is able to sail across their bows with speed*

Boat on boat

"To maximise the chance of hitting the 'racing line' around the mark in close company, start planning well ahead, thinking through the other boats' moves before they do."

Photo 11.7 74 flies her kite at a hot approach angle and just manages to sail around the pack's bows. 41 is sailing high to protect the inside: the "wiggle" will ensure that no-one has an inside overlap. Hull 04, behind 74, is overlapped by everyone. They either need to use the wiggle to break some overlaps, or slow and find a space to luff across the transoms of the boats inside, and exit next to the mark

Photo 11.8 41's wiggle gave them the inside berth. Hull 04 is still stuck on the outside. 75 is bearing away to create room for a tight rounding, while 51 made a late drop and is trying to find clear wind on the outside

Photo 11.9 74 is ahead out of shot. 75 made enough room to round tight on the mark. 51 is still sailing free to achieve a safe leeward position: they are committed to going right! 04's passive approach leaves them with no wind and no options

The gybe drop

The gybe drop (also known as a "Kiwi") around the port hand mark leaves all the options open.

Orange protects the left: all he will need is an overlap to pass a boat ahead. Until boats are about to round the mark, the starboard tack boat has right of way. Orange's approach at a big angle to the rest of the fleet leaves no argument about whether his overlap was established on time. Rule 18.4 allows him to sail all the way to his racing line before gybing. Rule 18.2d means that any boats overlapped outside have to keep clear through the whole gybe drop manoeuvre. Orange judges his layline so that there is room to gybe and drop before the actual rounding. In more wind his final layline is further to windward to allow time for the gybe and drop. And in a bag boat, the spinnaker comes down the right side for the next launch... perfect!

Fig 11.8 The gybe drop ("Kiwi")

"If the approach is a tight one, time to complete the drop will also be tight. In this case, gybe directly upwind of the mark. The dead run approach kills speed, so gives maximum time to get the kite in the bag. Conversely, if above the layline to the mark, gybe late to keep speed on for as long as possible, and approach the mark at a much "hotter" angle."

Photo 11.10 *A gybe directly upwind of the mark slows the boat and gives maximum time to drop and prepare for the beat*

The leeward gate

Many modern courses have a gate rather than a single leeward mark. We can use the table fig 1.13 (chapter 1 page 23), to give an indication of the gain available through bias alone. A 10 boat length width gate, with 10 degrees bias, gives around 4 boat lengths advantage to the biased end. (Two lengths on the run, two on the beat!)

"Now think about the other aspects: which way do we want to go up the next beat, and which mark are the boats ahead going for? A clear lane and one less tack at the unbiased end may easily negate this 4 boat length advantage."

Which end gives the most straightforward boat handling (both for the drop and the next hoist)? A gybe drop could make both leeward and windward mark kite handling simpler, and give more passing opportunities at each.

Choosing the "wrong" mark, with an early tack, could get us sailing the right way in a clear lane even when there is a pack of boats just ahead. But check the boats behind before choosing this option, which requires sailing back across any bad wind caused by the following pack (fig 11.9).

"And watch for fast increasing leverage: if we start 10 boat lengths apart and sail on opposite tacks for just 30 seconds, the total separation may already be approaching 30 boat lengths: we could be pretty vulnerable to a shift if everyone has gone the other way!"

Fig 11.9 *Though the shortest route is via the starboard mark, Mauve opts for a clear lane around the port mark. But if Mauve wants an early tack, he first checks for running boats behind!*

If rounding the starboard gate mark, it's even more important to hit the exit right on the layline. Boats slightly below the layline can't tack onto port tack without risking fouling the starboard tack boats behind and to windward (photo 11.11). A perfect starboard gate mark rounding can give control over a pack of boats ahead.

Photo 11.11 *Boats rounding the starboard gate mark need a perfect rounding if they want an early tack onto port*

COACH TOP TIP

- *Be prepared to slow down to break an outside overlap: slower is faster sometimes!*

- *Avoid establishing last minute overlaps, inside or outside: they cramp our style!*

- *If boats are close, drop the kite as soon as it's clear the overlap situation is not going to change. This gives more chance to prepare for the rounding, more space to clear the transoms of the boats ahead, and may force the boat just behind to establish an outside overlap: goodbye!*

- *Sheet the main on in time with the leeward mark turn to keep the sail driving; too soon will stall the sail.*

- *When manoeuvring closely, make sure the helm knows the situation at the front of the boat: both proximity to other boats and boat handling wise, using agreed language: "Clear to tack", "Clear to luff", "Clear to bear away".*

Off the wind, port tack has to give way to starboard tack only up to the point that boats are "about to round or pass a mark on the same side". At this point rule 18 takes over. Note that if sailing at high speed "about to round" could be interpreted as significantly more than 2 boat lengths from the mark (photo 11.14).

Photo 11.14 *Boats can be "about to round" well before 2 boat lengths*

If an inside overlap existed at two boat lengths, the inside boat retains rights even if the overlap is broken inside the circle. If the outside boat is not able to give room when an overlap is established, the inside boat is not entitled to room, even if the overlap was made before two boat lengths. This could happen for example in a large fleet, where it's simply not possible for all the boats outside to respond to a boat gaining a late overlap. "Room" is the space needed when "manoeuvring promptly in a seamanlike way". This may not necessarily allow the inside boat to follow the perfect racing line, unless the inside boat is also right of way boat.

Which rules apply?

Photo 11.12 *Read the rules!*

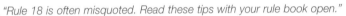 *"Rule 18 is often misquoted. Read these tips with your rule book open."*

Photo 11.13 *Rule 18 can apply between boats on opposite tacks*

A good leeward mark rounding provides the springboard for the next beat. A bad one means that strategy has to be overridden in the search for clear wind.

 "To make the most of the leeward mark, practise the manoeuvres until they are automatic, and watch out for the developing tactical opportunities rather than reacting to the actions of other boats."

Dealing with the handicap fleet

Not all of us who race sailboats have a class start, or even other boats of the same class to race against.

"Most of the principles discussed in this book apply equally to handicap racing, but I have picked up a few tips from the handicap and pursuit race gurus which might help you to navigate around the ultimate obstacle course!"

Keep out of trouble!

"If you read no further, write these four words down and repeat out loud whenever approaching a busy leeward mark!"

When sailing in a class fleet, it's obvious when an individual luffing or covering duel - or a log jam at a mark - is distracting us from the "big picture". In a handicap race, every boat length's diversion from the fastest route - and every unnecessary manoeuvre - is time given away to the faster or slower boats who may not even be visible at the time.

"Keep thinking: just how much time is a defensive manoeuvre going to waste, compared with sailing a low line and letting the faster boats pass quickly?

"If a bunch of faster boats is approaching as you round the windward mark, make an early detour well above or below the rhumb line so the faster boats can come by causing the minimum of distress. But whatever happens, don't get involved in a protracted luffing/covering match, unless you are sure that there are no other boats close on corrected time in the big race!"

Photo 12.1 *Watch out for bigger boats rounding behind*

Plan according to the class mix

"I ask myself: how big is our rig compared with the other boats I am starting with? If I'm sailing my Fireball against 505's or 14's, I feel that the overall effect of the wind being forced above and around the edges of the fleet has a major effect on my relatively small rig (fig 12.1). I therefore plan to get much closer to the sides of the course than I would in a single class start, even overstanding the windward mark if it is a big fleet. I always start near the end of the line, and sometimes even start on port tack at the starboard end if there is a gap, so I can get quickly to the side of the course. Playing the shifts up the middle of the course never seems to work for the smaller boats, whereas if I've got the biggest rig in the fleet, it's not such an issue.

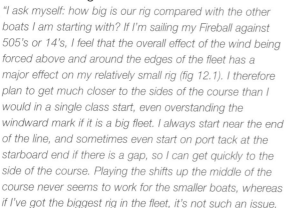

Fig 12.1 The wind is forced over and around the fleet. This will serious affect a shorter rigged boat starting in the middle of the line

"If I'm the fastest boat downwind, especially in an asymmetric boat, I'll avoid the middle of the run. The smaller boats are like obstacles, just waiting to slow you down. I'd rather gybe off and go the 'wrong way' down the run than try to weave a way through them.

"And to keep out of trouble means more than just knowing your rights. It's all very well approaching the leeward mark with rights but if the slower outside boat doesn't appreciate just how much room we need for a gybe/drop, it's going to be a mess. If he is going to wait until two boat lengths before he starts to react there is not going to be room: I'm better off dropping early, following him round, and explaining the rules another day!"

Think ahead, and remember your strategy.
Small boats are usually more manoeuvrable, and often faster to accelerate than bigger ones. But a perfect pin end start in a Solo/Mumm 30/Meleges 24 is no good if the RS 400's just squeeze up behind and to windward and prevent a tack over to the favoured right hand side. If our strategy is to avoid the main tide, it's even worse when they roll forward and give us dirty wind all the way to the slack tide on the left! (fig 12.2)

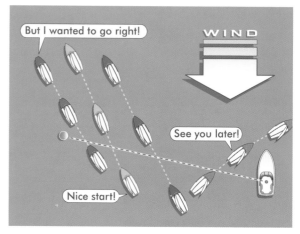

Fig 12.2 *Solo (Blue) forced left by the RS 400's*

"Sailing a slower boat, I apply the same basic rules as for a class race: check out the line, work out which side of the beat will be favoured. But I then look out for what the faster boats look like they are planning. I'd probably go for a slightly more conservative start so I don't get forced away from the 'right way'."

In pursuit races it is easy to get tied up in the battle with the boats in your fleet. But you do have to remember your overall goal: if it's to win the event not the class, your tactics have to be more bold: covering the Wayfarers into the strong tide in the middle of the channel may ensure a win in the fleet, but it won't help the race against time and handicap with the rest of the fleet. To win overall be prepared to be bold, and if ahead of the other boats in your class, keep pushing to maximise the other external effects (tide, wind bends, etc).

Photo 12.2 Remember the bigger picture!

Every second counts

In a class race, we tend to work harder at those manoeuvres when there are other boats nearby: we leave the spinnaker drop later trying to gain or break an overlap, we work hard on the perfect "wide in, tight out" rounding to give a small advantage over the boats around at the leeward mark. But if we are in a nice space, we'll make a more conservative drop, overstand the windward mark a little rather than risk two extra tacks, and so on. In handicap racing we can't afford to relax in this way: that overstand may be just enough for the Finns to beat us on handicap! Handicap races are often won and lost by seconds.

There is always an opportunity to save time at the finish line. If it is an upwind finish, try to establish which is the end of the line furthest from the wind.

"If the line looks easier to cross on port tack, the favoured end will be the starboard end!"

Aim to finish at that end, and depending on the weight of the boat, around 1 boat length from the line, luff to head to wind. A perfectly timed "shoot" of the line shortens the distance to sail to the finish, and can gain those vital seconds on corrected time.

The Moth factor

A hydrofoiling Moth is so much faster than every other boat on the water that an extreme defensive tactic is the only way to keep out of trouble.

"Don't bother shouting 'starboard': by the time they hear you it will be too late! Treat every other boat as if it is a stationary obstacle: your job is to find the most efficient way around the obstacles. And make sure that the race committee know where you are on the course: it's embarrassing to reach the finish line before they do!"

Photo 12.3 Don't even bother calling starboard!

Photo 12.4 *Find a clear lane downwind*

"In a fast asymmetric, my first concern is the class race you have with your own fleet - you have to win that to win the handicap race. But then there are the basic passing manoeuvres; climbing through the other classes efficiently can help with your own fleet struggle."

- *Very slow boats: take the shortest distance to get round them, windward or leeward, as you go past so much quicker the dirty air of a leeward pass has little or no effect.*
- *High pointing keel boats: Pass to leeward if approaching from astern or slightly to windward of the stern line. High pointers don't leave much dirt for faster low pointers. Trying to pinch round them to windward can be very slow.*
- *Large groups of slower boats: Avoid at all costs! Look well ahead and try and stay to one side of them. In light air the windward side is imperative.*
- *Approaching marks: If possible, try to plan the mark approach to get the inside berth: it is often easier for the bigger faster boats to sail through dirty air to this favoured position tactically. But in stronger winds not getting too involved is often the fastest way to the front.*
- *After the mark: Work out which is the favoured tack or gybe before you get there. If you want to 'gybe set' don't get to windward of a line of RS 200's! Look for a gap on the approach and slow down if necessary to get in it.*
- *Downwind: In a busy mixed fleet, finding a clean line where you can sail your boat to its optimum can be difficult. You have to look a long way down the course, and try to anticipate where the boats coming upwind are going, and where they might tack. This can be difficult if you are not all on the same course. A good rule of thumb is: if the tide is under you going downwind the boats coming up towards you will try and stay out of the channels, and visa versa. Fast asymmetric boats have a very narrow optimum downwind angle: the slightest luff above this angle and you are on your ear with no visibility, and sailing much further for little more speed. To bear away slightly from the optimum angle means huge deceleration and the apparent wind moves aft. So you end up slower and not much lower. The clean line down-wind can gain you many yards on boats in your class, and big chunks of time on handicap.*
- *Bear in mind how much faster you are sailing than the boats around. Sometimes you hold on too long before tacking, only to find when you do finally tack, you comfortably cross the boat you were worried about."*

Tacking, ducking and waving

There is little point in an Optimist trying to lee bow a Flying Fifteen, or a Melges 24 a Farr 40! The Fifteen will sail straight past, and deliver a big bag of dirty wind as it does so. But an Optimist which ducks a Flying Fifteen loses at least three boats' lengths: catastrophic compared with ducking another Oppie! Depending on the beating strategy, there are a couple of less painful alternatives:

- Sail high and slow: As soon as he knows he has to alter course, the slower boat sails high and slow for a couple of boat lengths. Rather than giving away distance, he has traded speed and gained a bit of height. As soon as it is clear that the big boat is clear, he resumes normal best upwind course (fig 12.3).
- Tack early: He tacks at least four boat lengths to leeward of the faster boat. If he chooses to keep going on starboard, the bad wind effect is much reduced. Alternatively he can tack back onto port before it even arrives.
- Wave them on: Though it may be very satisfying for an RS 400 to slow an Osprey down by calling starboard and forcing it to tack, it will hurt in the long run. Eventually the Osprey, with its big rig, will be up and running: it is not fast

enough to disappear before the lee bow effect starts to hurt. Unless the boat on starboard tack definitely wants to tack, a clear wave and early "carry on" call, and a duck of a couple of feet is much less painful. And the Osprey might return the favour next time round!

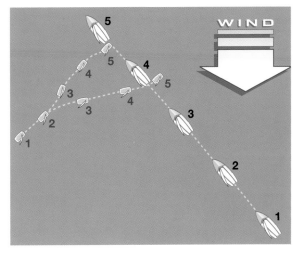

Fig 12.3 *The Optimist sails high and waits for the Fifteen to pass by, rather than giving away three Oppie boat lengths*

Know the angles

Every class has an ideal downwind running "vmg" angle, which may vary depending on wind strength. Lasers sail straight down the run, or even by the lee. Asymmetric boats sail much higher angles, which get deeper as the wind increases. When running in mixed fleets it is really important to be aware of the characteristics of the boats around, including the faster ones behind, and the slower ones ahead. For example, a Laser should always avoid getting stuck to windward of an RS 200. However the overlap was created, the Laser has to keep clear and will get forced off its fastest course, losing time against the clock. It's not in the RS's interest to get into this situation either: the spinnaker will collapse and it will take an age to get clear: all the time the clock is ticking!

Photo 12.5 *Each class has its own downwind angle*

Keep an eye on the clock

If we know how many minutes per hour our major competitors allow us (or we allow them) we can get a rough check on the overall situation half or three quarters the way through the race. By now, hopefully, the fleets are more spread out, and strategy becomes more than just finding clear lanes. If we look like we are well ahead, we might sail a little more conservatively: tacking (or gybing) before we hit the shallows, keeping a loose cover on the other boats in our fleet. If we are behind, we can push a little harder: we've nothing to lose! If it is close, remember that seconds mean places in handicap racing: a really slick spinnaker hoist, or a windward mark overstand, could make all the difference.

Photo 12.6 *At least you are sailing a boat that you like!*

"And never give up: even if your handicap calculations tell you that other classes have an advantage half way through the race, remember that a change in wind strength can easily negate this advantage. But if you do find yourself on the wrong side of everything, just go out and enjoy it! At least you are sailing a boat that you like!"

The final rounds

As the race develops, our objectives usually shift towards consolidating a good result, or recovering from a bad one. In this chapter we'll look at protecting our position, pulling through the fleet, and tactics on the finish line.

All the principles discussed so far apply to the equivalent leg, next time round. Hopefully, for those of us lucky enough to get a second chance, we can use lessons learnt on the first lap to adapt our strategy for the second.

"But beware: the fact that right paid on the first beat doesn't guarantee the same on the second: Kiel case study (chapter 4 page 56) gives one example of this phenomenon."

1 Protecting a position

"After the first few days of a sportsboat European championships in 2000, we had established a reasonable lead on points. But the conditions were tricky: light to medium winds, shifty and patchy, with no clear pattern. We found ourselves leading several of the subsequent races, but each time, the pack of boats immediately behind us was determined to split from the fleet of 75 or so chasing them. We agonised over loose covering the small chasing pack - giving a chance for us to win the race - or shadowing the body of the fleet. Each time, we covered the fleet, and, each time, one or two of the chasing pack pulled past us. But at the end of each day, our points lead had increased. None of the race winners were able to put together a consistent series; while our very conservative tactics built us a huge cushion of some 30 points by the final day."

There is more to protecting your position than "keeping between the next boat and the next mark". Choosing the right asset management strategy is fundamental to protecting a position.

Race objective:

What position are we trying to protect? In many cases, it's much more straightforward to take each race as it comes, rather than looking at every leg of every race in the context of a whole series. If we've won the first 5 races in a 10 race series, the strategy and tactics must be fairly sound. Sailing in an entirely different way just because we are now leading the race or series would be pointless. In contrast, as the regatta we've described developed, a healthy points lead and unpredictable conditions made shadowing the main fleet a safer long term bet than aiming for individual race wins.

First beat:

It's rare to be lucky enough to have a significant position to protect on the first beat. Getting involved too early with boat on boat tactics can seriously misfire. Unless the second leg is a close reach, a small lead at the windward mark is extremely vulnerable. Therefore the best way to protect a good position is to use any opportunity to extend: "more of the same!" A couple of simple principles may help us to maintain our advantage without giving it away.

In an oscillating breeze, Orange "banks" the gain by using his header to tack and cross ahead of, or at least reduce the separation on, the pack.

Now a right hand shift can't hurt him, he will sail on port or tack to loosely cover the pack depending on which way he expects the wind to shift next. In fig 13.2, he "banks" the gain from a header by sailing slightly fast and free, moving forward on the fleet and into that controlling position.

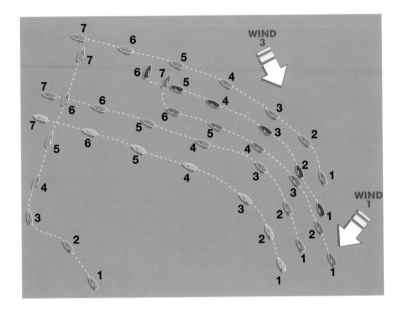

Fig 13.1 Orange "banks" the lift

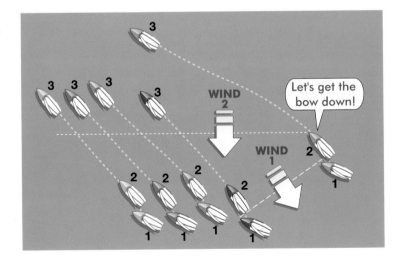

Fig 13.2 Orange banks the header

If the wind or current is persistently favouring one side of the beat, Orange makes sure that he uses the shifts to lead the fleet to the favoured side: either tacking ahead or to leeward of the pack to ensure he maintains the advantage. In fig 13.3, Orange tacks to leeward but ahead of the bulk of the fleet, which is to the right and below the figure. Yellow may make the biggest gain by hitting the left the hardest, but if the wind lifts, he will be out of touch with the fleet. If it doesn't, he'll probably get it wrong tomorrow!

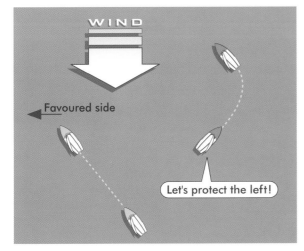

Fig 13.3 Orange leads the fleet to the favoured right hand side

The run:

A close cover on the beat gives the boat behind bad air: it doesn't work like that on the run. It's so easy to lose a hard won advantage on the run by sailing slightly too high, attempting to keep clear air from the boats behind. Inevitably we then get pinned out by them as they bring breeze down from behind. If we then gybe, they will gybe on top and grind down the distance even more. Sail to the layline, they will do the same, leave us with bad air all the way to the mark, and will also have inside advantage at the mark.

Photo 13.2 *Sailing to the layline gives boats behind an opportunity to attack on the gybe: the red gennaker has done just that*

Unless the run is very one sided in favour of starboard tack, an early gybe will maintain clear wind, and give the freedom to sail a strategic run. A good gybe, executed in an area of pressure, loses very little, and may even keep us in the gust for longer. Once clear of the predators from behind we can get back to strategic and tactical basics and work at accumulating small gains with no associated risk. Sail in the pressure, sail on the headers, and if in doubt, sail the longest gybe first. If the situation is close, protect the "inside side" of the run (for the mark rounding): that means any boats close by will have to sail right round and break an overlap to lead round the mark, rather than just establishing an inside overlap.

Cover or Extend?

As the race progresses, a close cover becomes more tempting. A close cover means that someone else makes the decisions. The trap we must not fall into, especially in shifty conditions, is to blindly cover the boat behind, irrespective of the wind we are sailing in. It's so easy for the covered boat(s) to time their tacks so they stay in phase, while we are permanently tacking onto headers. Slowly, the lead will be ground down. This may be OK on the last beat, as winning the race by six inches gets the same points as winning by a mile. But we should always be looking to extend where possible, without taking unnecessary risks. Extending will relieve the pressure on the forthcoming downwind legs, and make that last beat ever easier.

Loose cover:

We use the information gained throughout the race so far to protect the favoured side, while loosely watching and covering the fleet. A loose cover means we can sail to our own patches of wind, and tack as the shifts hit us, rather than letting the chasing pack dictate our tactics. If the fleet splits behind, it's sometimes possible to "herd" them back together (chapter 7). If this isn't possible, and the series result is more important than the individual race win, we may just let the radical movers take their chance, and accept that they may win a race but they won't win the regatta. Whatever our decision, we keep looking upwind, keep sailing fast, and try to keep doing the things which got us here in the first place.

"Use the small shifts to reduce leverage from the fleet where possible, aim to always be further advanced along the long leg if the beat is skewed, and of course keep inside the shift lines."

We use a loose cover to manage our risk, by minimising the leverage achieved by our nearest competitor, or group of competitors. Meanwhile we can work out how to get past the next group of boats. When loose covering, we deliberately avoid sitting directly on the competition's wind to slow them down, as this would encourage them to tack away to a different part of the course.

Fig 13.4 *Orange establishes a classic loose cover*

Orange (fig 13.4) has a 10 boat length lead over Mauve, in the chasing pack. One way she can establish a safe loose cover position is by tacking after she's sailed about a third of this distance, when, for example she is three or four boat lengths from the mark. Orange then tacks back onto starboard as Mauve makes her final approach to the mark. Mauve rounds the mark straight into a loose cover situation. Orange deliberately leaves Mauve's wind free. Her objective is to stay in touch and in phase with the shifts, rather than to force Mauve into a series of tacks in an attempt to gain clear wind, which would slow both down. She could have achieved this by tacking slightly early to be more advanced. She chooses the alternative "safe windward" cover. This more windward position means that if Mauve tacks, Orange is not rushed into a quick tack in response, to maintain the loose cover. She can check the wind bearing, check the other boats, pick her spot, and still make a controlled tack, in plenty of time to achieve that all important psychological bow-forward controlling position (fig 13.5).

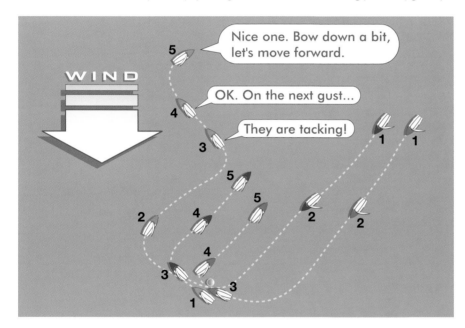

Fig 13.5 *Orange's positioning avoids the need for a rushed tack*

If Mauve does not tack, and the wind seems to be heading into the left hand corner, Orange may begin to feel a little vulnerable out to windward. In this case she simply eases sheets one click, and sails fast for a few boats' lengths to re-establish the bow forward position.

- Pick the right spot to tack: The key to managing a loose cover is not to get rushed. Be aware of the wave and wind patterns, and find a nice heading gust to tack in. If necessary, sail fast and free once the tack is complete to re-establish the bow forward position.
- Stay between the fleet and the next shift: If a lift is impending, sail high to gain maximum impact when it arrives. If a header is imminent, sail fast and free, getting the bow forward over the fleet to leeward, and reducing the leverage.
- "Stay between the fleet and the next mark." This sounds obvious, but it's easy to get carried away and sail past the layline, allowing the competition to reach through to leeward. If the covered pack is continuing to edge off the course, the coverer can sail high and slow for a while as the layline approaches. This gives them a slightly bow forward position, putting more pressure on them to pick the layline. Once the covered boats tack for the mark, the coverer can increase his lead by tacking directly ahead and sailing less distance.
- If the fleet splits up, use herding tactics (chapter 9) to encourage them back together.

Close cover:

If, despite our best sailing, and mature tactics, the boat immediately behind still threatens to pass, then the most offensive "sit on their face", close cover may be the only solution.

A close cover ensures that the only wind the opposition receives has come straight through our mainsail, and also means that the only way they can pass is to physically sail through our boat. It's the only way to deal with a boat close behind with superior boatspeed, but even professional America's Cup sailors struggle to keep it up for more than a leg.

Close cover tactics are also used to achieve specific outcomes. A close tack on a competitor's wind at the windward mark layline before the start of the run might give that extra boat length's breathing space for the hoist. Championship results can be turned around on the last beat, simply through one competitor covering another back to a poor position in the final race of the series.

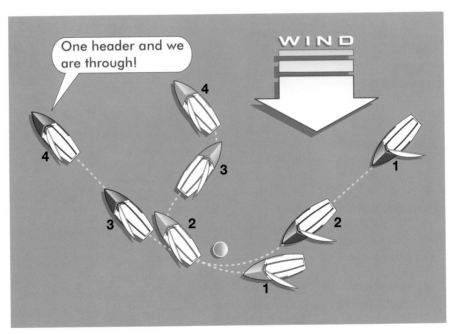

Fig 13.6 *At this distance, Orange's two tacks put him into a vulnerable position*

The distance between boats in a close cover situation is 4-5 boats' lengths maximum. Putting two extra tacks in at the start of the beat could easily compromise this lead (fig 13.6). Instead, Orange has two options.

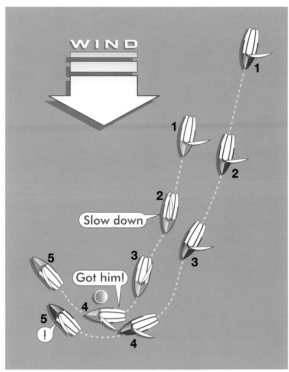

Fig 13.7 Orange forces Mauve to round outside into a close cover position

In fig 13.7, as soon as Orange is confident that Mauve cannot establish an inside overlap, he slows his boat. A nice early spinnaker drop, a gybe without flicking the battens, a short period of sailing by the lee. The objective is to ensure that Mauve rounds the mark with an overlap. The beat begins with Mauve both gassed and pinned, unable to tack clear.

In fig 13.8, Mauve makes his normal smooth rounding, but luffs hard (not past head to wind; see rule 13) as soon as he is clear of the mark. Pink has no chance: she either misses Mauve's transom by ducking, or by luffing straight into a tack. Either way Mauve gains the close cover: if Pink tacks, Mauve simply continues the luff into a perfect cover tack (Fig 13.9).

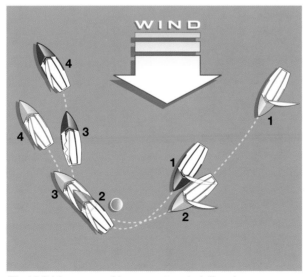

Fig 13.8 Mauve uses his momentum to luff and gain a tight cover

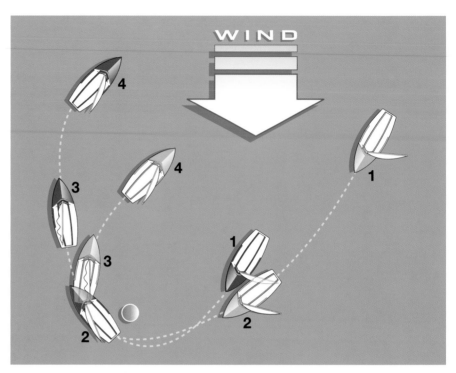

Fig 13.9 *If Pink tacks, Mauve turns his luff into a covering tack*

Establishing a close cover when part way up the beat.

So far, Orange has sailed a reasonable beat, keeping in phase with the shifts. Mauve has found some extra breeze to the right, and made a gain, though port is currently the lifted tack. Mauve attempts to tack into a close cover: Orange simply tacks too. Now Orange is on the lift, and heading back into the breeze! Next time they cross he'll be even closer!

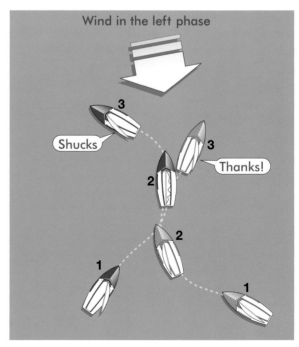

Fig 13.10 *Mauve's attempted cover simply sends Orange the way he wants to go*

So what could Mauve do?

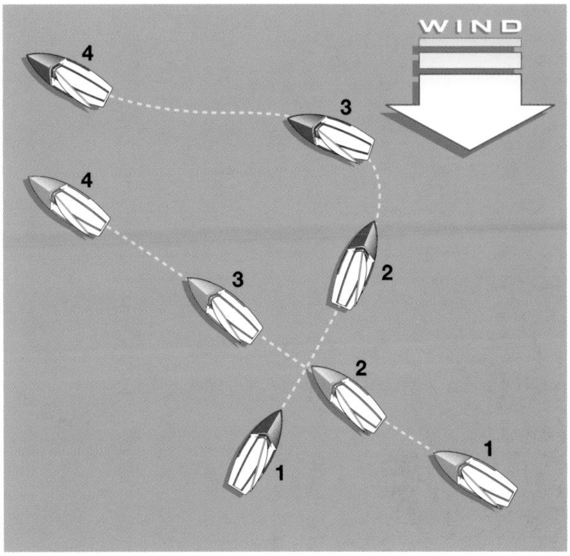

- Tack into a safe windward position first (fig 13.11). If Orange isn't initially affected, he may not tack off. In this case, Mauve can turn a safe windward into a close cover by sailing free and fast. Now if Orange tacks, Mauve can tack too, and will remain on Orange's wind, and lead to the favoured side. If Orange had tacked immediately, Mauve's extra couple of boats' lengths to the right may have given him time to get back to speed, and tack back into a safe windward on port tack.
- Keep in touch with the oscillations. While this in-fighting occurs, it's easy to lose touch with shifts. If Mauve chooses not to play, he must make sure his last tack is onto the favoured (in this case port) tack.
- Protect the favoured side. In this case, Mauve should aim to maintain the advantage by delaying his tack onto starboard through each phase of the duel, gaining leverage on the favoured side. As with herding, whenever Orange is on port tack, Mauve tacks right on Orange's wind. When he's on starboard, Mauve delays his tack slightly, and allows himself a little leverage.
- Try a dummy. Mauve should watch Orange's reaction as Mauve starts his first tack onto starboard. If Orange is over eager with his response, Mauve could simply abort the tack and immediately gain his close cover position.
- Slam Dunk. Orange (fig 13.12) begins her tack during Pink's ducking manoeuvre. Pink luffs back to close hauled, to find Orange right on her wind, too close to allow a tack to freedom. In practice, this is a high risk manoeuvre. In a match race there would be a jury boat to confirm that Orange complied with Rules 16.2, 13, and 11. In a normal fleet race, he would have to convince either Pink, or the protest committee. In any case, unless Orange's tack is anything but perfect, she'll complete the tack struggling to accelerate, in danger of Pink's lee bow effect.

Fig 13.11 Mauve turns a safe windward position into a tight cover

When truly close covering, there are no half measures. The gap between the boats is too close to allow the leeward boat any chance to attack. "Tacking on their face" means just that. If the leeward boat sails fast and free, trying to get bow forward, the windward boat must do the same. If he tacks, the windward boat tacks and re-establishes position on his wind. Watch the covered boat's tiller or wheel and follow its movements. That way you'll never be sold a dummy. While this is all happening, someone on your boat needs to be keeping an eye on the rest of the fleet: at some stage it may be necessary to break off the one-on-one game and return to the real race.

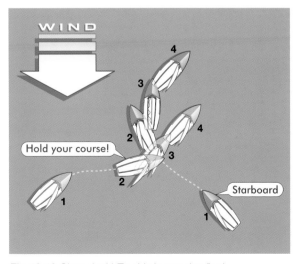

Fig 13.12 Slam dunk! Try this in practice first!

The final beat:

- How safe is our lead, and how long the beat?
- How far behind the second boat is the rest of the pack?
- Is our boat handling as good as the boats just behind?
- How confident are we of the wind conditions?
  The answers to these questions will determine whether we opt to sail our own race, continue with a loose cover, or decide to pin a close cover on one or more boats on the final beats.

Don't panic!

"If I'm good enough to get to the front, I'm good enough to stay there. And if our tactics and strategy were good enough to win the first beat, they are probably good enough to win the race. Gaps will always reduce and enlarge through a race, and the most successful asset managers are those who stay cool, making the most of the peaks, on order to be able to ride the dips.

"Never lose sight of opportunities to extend: if we allow our lead to steadily erode through totally defensive sailing, that winning position could eventually be lost through one mistake; a fluffed tack, a botched spinnaker hoist, and so on.

"The best defenders always combine their covering tactics with a willingness to make the most of any safe opportunity to increase a lead."

2 Pulling through the fleet

"In the last, non-discardable race of Kiel Week, our crew needed a good result to improve their 4th place standing, and challenge the world youth champion's overall supremacy in the regatta. Both teams came off the line in good shape, and sailed towards the breeze on the left, separating from the body of the fleet by only 20 boat lengths or so. The wind then unexpectedly dropped to nothing and shifted hard right, leaving them buried in the bottom half of the fleet. Here is the British team's description of their recovery:-

"We said to ourselves, let's just have a bit of fun, and see how many boats we can pass. For the rest of the first beat, we used every little header to tack towards the next small bit of pressure, just trying to gain the distance back boat length by boat length. Inevitably, we got to the layline earlier than we'd have liked to maintain clear wind, but

keeping to the right on the windward mark approach did keep us away from the dirty wind of the reaching boats who had rounded ahead. Once on the layline, we worked really hard on fast forward speed, and managed to sail around a couple of boats fighting against each other on or below the layline. We rounded the windward mark in the 20's, with lots still to do.

"Though the fleet was mainly sailing above the rhumb line on the reach, we stuck to our game plan which was to sail up for the pressure, get into the passing lane high enough to avoid being luffed, then hoist the kite and roll the boats to leeward in less pressure, one by one. All we were thinking about was; 'how can we gain the boat lengths on the boats immediately ahead?' We were not trying to pass the whole fleet by sailing a great circle route. Rather than worry about our position in the fleet, we were just thinking about making small gains on the group of boats ahead; once in touch 'how we can pass them?'; then accumulating small gains on the next bunch, and so on.

"The champ took the low route on the reach and looked very good at one stage, but we continued to sail high for the next gust, then once in it take it down, with enough speed to roll the next boat.

"We gybed down the middle of the run, focussing on sailing the bands of pressure, again chipping away all the time. Occasionally someone right out one side would look good, but we didn't worry about the individuals, knowing that their chance of keeping the breeze all the way back to the mark would be minimal. By now we were up into the teens, and back in the race proper. Around 10 boats' lengths from the mark, we decided that there was more pressure on the left (looking upwind) side of the bottom of the course, so we worked our way to the right side of the fleet at the bottom of the run to make a tight rounding of the starboard hand gate mark.

"Luckily the fleet around made for the other mark which left us space for a nice clean rounding. One of the positive points about an unexpected shift on the first beat is that there is likely to be a lower standard than usual at the front!

"We watched the leaders up the beat get headed on starboard, and though it looked as if the wind might continue to head and increase we decided to bank our

gain by tacking back onto port back towards the centre of the beat. The champ actually kept going and hit the left hand side quite hard; we did get lifted and lifted on port, though the next band of wind started to come from the right: if this had come sooner he would have been stuck right out on the left hand side of the beat on his own. The last part of the beat was really shifty: by staying away from the laylines we were able to take advantage of the shifts and pass a couple more boats on each side, rounding the windward mark 4th, with the champ 3rd, and German teams first and second.

"Following the same conservative game on the run enabled us to pass one of the Germans, and close on the leading two. By the end of the run, the champ was close behind the leading German with a fair gap back to us in third. While they spent the final reach sailing high, playing games with each other, we sailed as fast as we could down the rhumb line; we knew we couldn't pass them on this leg , but wanted to get close enough to attack them on the last beat.

"There were three shifts on this last tiny beat, we got all three right, passed the German, and had a match race with our rival to the finish who finally beat us by about an inch!"

Stay Positive:
Consistent regatta winners have the skills to recover from a bad first beat without gambling everything on one shift. The first lesson we can learn from the story above is that thinking positive helps to us maintain the drive to recover.

"If we feel 'we may as well go home, then', or 'this will be our discard, anyway', it will be, and we may as well!"

But "let's see how many boats we can pass", or "what we can learn about this venue", are positive thoughts which give the rest of the race a point and a focus for enjoyment. With this positive attitude, clawing through the fleet is simply a rewarding way to test and improve our basic racing skills: strategy, boatspeed, and boat on boat tactics.

One bite at a time:
We will be very lucky to gain all the places back in one go. Both upwind and downwind, the route to success is through keeping focused on sailing the boat fast and in the right direction to reduce the gaps on the boats ahead, then using boat on boat or boat on fleet tactics to pass the individual boats or small bunches of boats. A second or two gained in each tack over the race might add up to several places by the end, add to this some gains on clean mark roundings, hoists, gybes, etc, and we are already on the road to recovery.

Learn from the mistakes:
As we approach the windward mark after a poor beat, we need to work out what went wrong with the strategy, and put this right. Were we simply forced to sail out of phase with the shifts after a bad start, or was there a wind bend, more pressure, or less tide on one side of the beat which we didn't notice? Were we on the outside of a persistent shift and is this likely to keep going, or were we genuinely unlucky? Sorting this out will help us not only improve our performance on the next beat, but also plan our strategy for the offwind legs.

"If we were out of phase with oscillating shifts, we make sure that we are on the headed gybe first on the run. If there was more pressure or a wind bend on one side of the course, let's look at hedging towards that side on the run. That's information we rarely get when we are in the leading pack!"

The first beat:
Look out for the lanes: After a bad start, tacking immediately on to port tack will often get us to a clear lane quicker. But we have to be sure that we are not going to have to duck the whole fleet, sail for too long on a headed shift, or be forced out to the wrong side of the beat. It may be better to sail with more twist, fast and free, take our medicine, and watch for a lane to appear ahead as the boats battling for the front rank are forced to tack away. If we do tack early onto port, but want to sail the left hand side of the beat, tacking back safely to windward of another starboard tacker will prevent a close lee bow from another port tacker. Again, looking up the course at the patterns of boats will make it easier to spot a clear lane to the favoured side.

Photo 13.3 *When behind it's tempting to split with the pack*

Photo 13.4 *...but there is usually a good reason that the rest of the fleet went left!*

The windward mark:

The windward mark is a great opportunity to make gains. The leaders often tack on the layline, the boats just behind over lay a little to keep clear wind, and so on until the boats at the back are reaching in from a great height. Not only have they sailed extra distance in dirty wind, they have missed any shifts in the last phase of the beat. In medium winds, a port tack approach at around four or five boats' lengths usually avoids this great circle route, and a gap to tack in often appears. Even if the port tack approacher has to sail through the line of starboard boats and tack to windward, he has only sailed a couple of boats' lengths extra and has held clear wind all the way to the layline.

In lighter wind this port tack approach may not be feasible: there may be right of way running boats already round the mark to negotiate, or a big patch of dead wind under the leaders on the first reach. If there is adverse tide, there may be a big group of boats stuffing and sailing slowly on starboard at the mark, in which case a high and fast approach may reap rewards. If the boats ahead aren't laying, an early tack into clear wind and a wide rounding with speed will get us through the bunch and onto the tail of the next one. Keep an open mind, watch the situation ahead, and take advantage of opening opportunities, while setting up for the right side of the first offwind leg.

Tight reach:

The low route rarely pays, unless the combination of a luffing match ahead plus no boats immediately behind has cleared the path sufficiently to allow an early undisturbed hoist and a route to a clear leeward lane. The danger is that if the breeze is coming down in patches, boats to windward will pick up and come down and forwards in the gusts.

In patchy conditions, or if there is no clear route through, the safer route is to sail high early enough to discourage the leeward boats from defending by luffing. At this distance we should be fast enough to roll them if they try. Good technique, the right equipment, and a high and sustained work rate will close the gap on the boats ahead, and pull us over those to leeward. As the reaching mark approaches, we use the acceleration for each little gust to bear off, roll the boat to leeward, and make sure we hit the two boats' length circle clear ahead.

The broad reach:

"Avoid the great circle route" is the key on the broad reach. As the fleet gets dragged further and further to windward of the rhumb line, it should now be easier to find a leeward lane early and use any gusts or waves to break clear to leeward. At this stage we definitely don't want to get involved in battles with individual boats.

The run:

By regularly watching upwind before the run begins, it's often possible to see the patterns or bands of wind. Sailing in the biggest pressure is usually the highest priority on the run, followed by sailing on the headers, but we can take into account anything we have learned upwind in planning the run. If we were lifted on the starboard tack approach to the mark, an early gybe is probably indicated. At the front of the fleet, an early gybe takes us into the disturbed wind below the starboard layline; this isn't a problem further down the fleet. In non-planing conditions, the leaders are often prevented from gybing onto port by the boats just behind, who have sacrificed a little speed to gain ground to leeward and establish the controlling position. This speed loss enables the boat behind to do exactly the same to him. Everyone is slowing down, trying to soak enough to break out of this destructive circle. Soon a boat rounds the mark, ignores the "soakathon" and sails to windward of the leaders, slowing them further. However he is not able to gybe away either!

If we spot this situation developing ahead, we should ensure that no one behind can get their bow below us as we round the windward mark. Now we can roll straight into a gybe (watching out for port tackers who are still coming up the beat). We're now sailing our own course with no interference from the pack around.

As the patches of wind roll down the course, we keep looking behind for the next one. Usually, when a gust begins to fade and lift, it's time to gybe back into its centre.

If there is a gate at the bottom of the mark, we pick the one which is furthest upwind unless there is a good reason (big traffic, big hole) to avoid it. Both run and beat will be shorter. We start to work towards the inside well before the leeward mark approach: it's a lot easier to get an overlap on a group of boats than to sail all the way around the outside and break an overlap.

The last beat:

"Don't give up" is the motto on the last beat. Everyone else is getting tired and thinking about the bar. As boats are more spread out, lanes should be easier to find. A "go the opposite way to everyone else" tactic is more likely to undo all the good work done so far, while playing the favoured side, keeping in phase with the shifts, keeping boatspeed up, and closing the gaps, will maintain the forward momentum.

Photo 13.5 *Never ever give up: especially in light winds*

Once across the line, "well done" to everyone on the boat, whatever the final result: every boat passed after a poor start or a poor first beat is a success: carrying these successes to the next race ensures we start it with the right positive attitude.

Breaking cover

We've looked at using tight and loose cover to protect our position. But what if the boot is on the other foot? Every time we think we have found a lane with some clear wind, the competition dumps on us: Whenever we try to gain a little leverage on the favoured side of the beat, the boats ahead shadow us.

"In any boat on boat situation it is vital to remain focused on overall beat strategy and windshift phase. The relief at gaining clear wind is otherwise soon replaced by the harsh realisation that we are sailing on the headed shift or into unfavourable tide while our rival increases his lead."

Don't let it happen

It's easier to avoid being covered than to break out of a close cover situation. If we suspect that a crossing boat is likely to "put one on us", we must prepare for the situation in advance: "If he weren't there, would we rather be on port or on starboard?" If we are expecting a header, or we are sailing towards the favoured side of the beat, we don't want to tack. If we are already headed, or sailing away from the favoured side, we may be very happy to tack, and even happier if the opposition goes the other way.

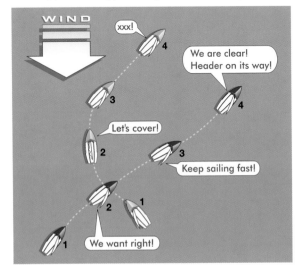

Fig 13.13 Mauve sails fast and free to avoid Pink's close cover

We don't want to tack

In this case Mauve needs to be in front of Pink's dirty wind zone by the time Pink has completed his tack and is up to speed. Often it's obvious what is about to happen next. Once Pink has crossed his line, Mauve sails fast and free. By the time Pink completes his tack, Mauve has moved forward to the safe position (fig 13.13). When the header comes, his right hand leverage will give him a small gain, and his grind back into contention has begun.

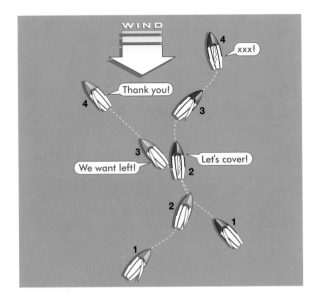

Fig 13.14 Orange times his clearing tack to prevent the close cover on starboard tack

We do want to tack

Orange's three concerns in this case are: using the conditions to make the best possible tack, avoiding the double tack, and spotting the dummy. Whatever Mauve's response, Orange must pick the right wind and wave conditions to pull off a perfect tack (fig 13.14). A gain of a couple of feet in this situation can make the difference between break through or more painful bad air. The sooner Orange tacks, the less likely that Mauve will be able to pull off a second tack in time to maintain close cover. But if Orange shows his hand too soon, Mauve simply turns his tack into a dummy, and achieves the perfect cover with little or no speed loss (fig 13.15). Orange watches the conditions, picks his spot, and only commits once he is certain that Mauve has also committed. If Orange spots Mauve rolling into a double tack, he sails fast and free for the safe position, just as in fig 13.13.

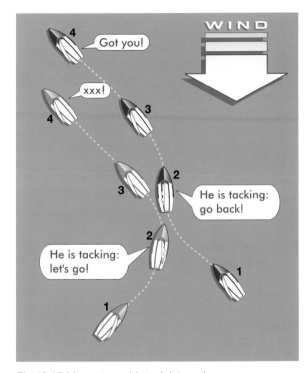

Fig 13.15 Mauve turns his tack into a dummy

It's most important with each of these options to anticipate and act decisively. If we wait until the other boat has achieved his cover, we'll start to lose ground straight away, and will have to use "wipe off" or "grind them down" (see p172).

Slam dunk. In many boat types and sailing conditions, this is not as easy a manoeuvre as it looks on paper. In small boat sailing it's more likely to be used to achieve a "pin" - sailing the other boat to the layline - rather than a true close cover.

Pink is sailing towards the starboard layline as Orange approaches. As Pink ducks, Orange tacks. Orange knows he won't achieve a close cover, but he can now pin Pink out to just beyond the layline, and guarantee that he rounds first, after slowing Pink all the way along the starboard tack approach. Pink has three options to break ranks; the correct choice will depend on wind shift phase, distance to the lay line, and distance from the windward mark, and the particular boat characteristics. (See photo sequence windward 11-16, p112)

- Keep out of trouble: Pink can avoid the issue by tacking early into a safe leeward position, on starboard, far enough from Orange to enable a tack back at will.

- Keep the options open: Pink can achieve the safe leeward position by reaching hard as Orange tacks. He creates a gap to windward big enough to avoid the pin.

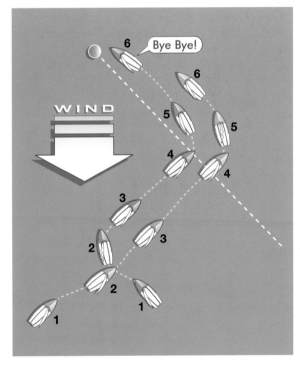

Fig 13.16 Orange tacks to pin Pink to the layline

- Break through: (fig 13.17) The most satisfying counter to an attempted pin or slam dunk is to achieve a reversal. Orange ducks early so that as he starts to cross Mauve's transom, he is already back on a close hauled course but with additional speed gained from the controlled close reach approach. As Mauve begins his tack, Orange uses this speed to luff and close the distance between the boats. Mauve completes his tack unable to bear off to gain speed. With luck Orange's bow wave creates additional problems for Mauve. Orange sails a high close hauled course, rolls the boat upright, or to windward if possible, and really works hard to make the lee bow hurt. A well executed reversal will result in Mauve being forced to make a slow tack with no speed back onto starboard, simply to avoid drifting sideways into Orange. Next time the boats cross Orange will be ahead and in control.

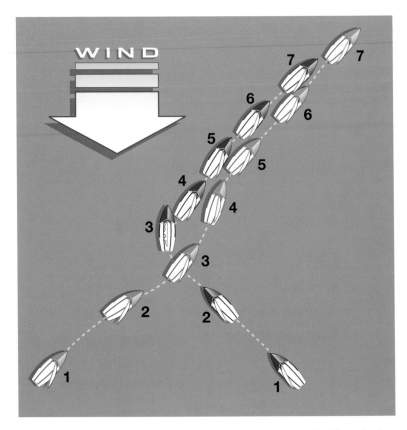

Fig 13.17 Orange gains speed then luffs to turn Mauve's slam dunk into a lee bow

At the leeward mark

It is occasionally possible to break cover if the boat ahead makes a poor rounding, by sailing fast and free through to the safe leeward position (photo 13.6). This is rarely successful in small boats unless there are extreme conditions: very light, very windy, lots of tide, lots of boats, or an especially bad rounding. When this manoeuvre works, it's generally opportunistic rather than planned. More conventionally, the two ways to break cover at the leeward mark are to dummy, or to tack.

The dummy tack works more often at the leeward mark than on the open course, because the crew of the boat ahead are often focussed on other things: tidying up, traffic, getting the boat up to speed. A perfect dummy has to be executed just as would on a normal tack; shouting "ready about" very loudly and standing up or uncleating the jib sheets in a meaningful way just doesn't convince. The most important point about the dummy is that if the covering boat doesn't react, the tack must be followed through; otherwise we have lost speed and distance and gained nothing. So we don't try a dummy if the tack would take us into the middle of the running pack, or into the wind shadow of another boat.

Photo 13.6 *The outside route may work if the inside rounding is bad*

Tips for dummies

- Only instigate a dummy tack if you are willing to continue onto the new tack.
- Set up and execute exactly as for a normal tack: "watch for a dummy" should be the only quiet warning.
- The whole crew should watch the tiller or wheel through the tack: this is the only indicator needed to confirm whether the tack will be completed or not.
- One person only watches the tiller or wheel of the other boat, ideally the helmsman.
- The helmsman only reverses the helm when the other boat is fully committed. It may be necessary to back the jib and heel to windward to help the boat back through the wind onto the old tack.
- Ease jib, twist main, sail free to get the boat back to speed as soon as possible, and minimise effect of any double tack from the competition.
- If successful, just give the competition a little wave, to remind them not to have the audacity to try to cover you again.

Wipe off

Boats on other tacks, obstructions, and congested lanes can be used as obstacles to "wipe off" the covering boat. We tack into a position that gives us a clear, free lane, but requires the other boat to hit the obstruction, duck the other boat, sail in dirty wind, or delay his covering tack. At worse we'll achieve Mauve's safe leeward position (fig 13.13, p168); at best the competition will be on the other tack or trying to dislodge himself from the boat or obstruction he has hit.

Grind them down

As well as using some of the techniques suggested to split tacks or clear our wind, we continue to take every opportunity to keep the pressure on the covering boat. These techniques are also used in loose cover situations, to narrow the gap and give an opportunity for a breakthrough.

- Make each tack pay. If possible, we want to make each tack perfect, on a smooth patch of water, in phase with the shifts, with a nice lifting gust to help us to accelerate out of the tack. Meanwhile, we try to time our tacks so that the competition makes a rushed tack, in choppy water and a lull, and comes out on a header with another boat on his wind! If we are in phase with all or some of these points, the chances are that the competition won't be. Each time, we gain a few yards.

- Avoid the laylines. Hitting the layline early gives us no escape route if the competition wants to be mean. Keeping well inside the laylines opens up our options.

- Keep focus on the overall race strategy. If there is an opportunity, get bow forward when heading towards the favoured side. Getting drawn into a one on one battle is an easy way to lose big distance and many places.

The finish

There is always a favoured end of the line, and there are frequently opportunities to gain places as a result. On an upwind finish, the favoured end of the line is the one which is furthest downwind (the opposite end to the one we'd start at). Just as with the start, that may not be the one which looks closest to the leeward mark. If the line was set square to the average wind direction, the left hand end is favoured if the wind is right of the mean, the right hand end if it is left. Ideally, we approach the line on the lifted tack,

then (depending on the weight of the boat) start to luff when about a boat length from the line. That will get our bow to the line sooner. If we are approaching on the headed tack, tacking to cross the line achieves the same effect.

On a run, the most upwind end is favoured; we'd make for the same end as we would choose for an upwind start. Again, rolling into a gybe might get the bow over the line those vital two seconds earlier.

Photo 13.7 *Aim for the upwind end of the line, and roll into a gybe to cross it at right angles to save those vital seconds*

On a reaching finish, there is always a balance between the shortest course, and the fastest course. The favoured end will depend on the wind strength, reaching angle, line angle, and boat characteristics. It's easy to defend from a boat trying to pass to windward by luffing: at this stage unless we are handicap racing we can take all the time we like so long as we get our bow across the line first. If there are two boats ahead which are luffing to windward of the rhumb line, there is always an opportunity to sail the straight line to the leeward end of the line.

The debrief

The race is over, the sandwiches come out. Whatever the result, a well meant "well done" to everyone on the boat sets the tone for a constructive debrief, and a positive outlook on the next race.

"Start with the positives: everyone must have done at least one thing well! With everyone feeling positive, 'what did we learn from the conditions, what worked, what didn't work, and what can we improve on?'

"'We were unlucky, we were slow, we were rubbish' are unhelpful conclusions. If we were unlucky, what can we do to reduce our exposure next time? If slow, what can we do before the next race (or the next regatta) to put that right?

"If we really were rubbish, I can recommend a good coach!

"Learning from a successful race is just as important. Identifying the race winning moves, or decisions resulting in significant gains, and the process which led to them will mean that we are more likely to repeat them next time."

Promoting and Protecting Boating

www.rya.org.uk

RYA Membership

Promoting and Protecting Boating

The RYA is the national organisation which represents the interests of everyone who goes boating for pleasure.

The greater the membership, the louder our voice when it comes to protecting members' interests.

Apply for membership today, and support the RYA, to help the RYA support you.

Benefits of Membership

- Access to expert advice on all aspects of boating from legal wrangles to training matters
- Special members' discounts on a range of products and services including boat insurance, books, videos and class certificates
- Free issue of certificates of competence, increasingly asked for by everyone from overseas governments to holiday companies, insurance underwriters to boat hirers

- Access to the wide range of RYA publications, including the quarterly magazine
- Third Party insurance for windsurfing members
- Free Internet access with RYA-Online
- Special discounts on AA membership
- Regular offers in RYA Magazine
- ...and much more

Join now - membership form opposite

Join online at *www.rya.org.uk*

Visit our website for information, advice, members' services and web shop.

1 Important To help us comply with Data Protection legislation, please tick *either* Box A or Box B (you must tick Box A to ensure you receive the full benefits of RYA membership). The RYA will not pass your data to third parties.

☐ **A.** I wish to join the RYA and receive future information on member services, benefits (as listed in RYA Magazine and website) and offers.

☐ **B.** I wish to join the RYA but do not wish to receive future information on member services, benefits (as listed in RYA Magazine and website) and offers.

When completed, please send this form to: RYA, RYA House, Ensign Way, Hamble, Southampton, SO31 4YA

2

Title	Forename	Surname	Date of Birth		Male	Female
1.			DD / MM / YY		☐	☐
2.			DD / MM / YY		☐	☐
3.			DD / MM / YY		☐	☐
4.			DD / MM / YY		☐	☐

Address

Town   County   Post Code

Evening Telephone   Daytime Telephone

email

3 Type of membership required: *(Tick Box)*

☐ ***Personal*** *Annual rate £37 or £34 by Direct Debit*

☐ ***Under 21*** *Annual rate £12 (no reduction for Direct Debit)*

☐ ***Family**** *Annual rate £56 or £52 by Direct Debit*

* Family Membership: 2 adults plus any under 21s all living at the same address

4 Please tick ONE box to show your main boating interest.

☐ Yacht Racing	☐ Yacht Cruising
☐ Dinghy Racing	☐ Dinghy Cruising
☐ Personal Watercraft	☐ Inland Waterways
☐ Powerboat Racing	☐ Windsurfing
☐ Motor Boating	☐ Sportsboats and RIBs

Signature: _____ Date: _____

Please see Direct Debit form overleaf

![RYA logo]

Instructions to your Bank or Building Society to pay by Direct Debit

Please complete this form and return it to:
Royal Yachting Association, RYA House, Ensign Way, Hamble, Southampton, Hampshire SO31 4YA

DIRECT Debit

To The Manager: _____ Bank/Building Society

Address: _____

Post Code: _____

2. Name(s) of account holder(s)

_____

3. Branch Sort Code

☐ ☐ — ☐ ☐ — ☐ ☐

4. Bank or Building Society account number

☐ ☐ ☐ ☐ ☐ ☐ ☐ ☐

Banks and Building Societies may not accept Direct Debit instructions for some types of account

Originators Identification Number

9	5	5	2	1	3

5. RYA Membership Number (For office use only)

_____

6. Instruction to pay your Bank or Building Society

Please pay Royal Yachting Association Direct Debits from the account detailed in this instruction subject to the safeguards assured by The Direct Debit Guarantee.

I understand that this instruction may remain with the Royal Yachting Association and, if so, details will be passed electronically to my Bank/Building Society.

Signature(s) _____

Date _____

Office use / Centre Stamp

Cash, Cheque, Postal Order enclosed £ _____

Made payable to the Royal Yachting Association

Office use only: Membership Number Allocated

077

Backed wind	Wind direction has moved anticlockwise
Bear away	Turn the boat downwind
Beat	Sailing upwind
Close cover	A boat is closely covering another by sailing upwind on the same tack, with the second boat in the first's wind shadow
Convergence	When the wind is parallel to the coast from the west the land causes the wind to back creating a band of strong wind close to the coast (northern hemisphere)
Course skew	The beat or run is offset to the wind direction
Cunningham	A sail's luff tension control
Current	Water flowing in a given direction
Dipping	Bearing away to cross behind another boat (ducking)
Discard	A race result dropped form a series overall score
Divergence	When the wind is parallel to the coast from the east the land causes the wind to back creating an area of less wind close to the coast (northern hemisphere)
Ducking	Bearing away to cross behind another boat (dipping)
Foils	Rudder blades, daggerboards, centreboards, keels
Gybe drop ('Kiwi')	The gybe and spinnaker drop are performaed simultaneously with the sail stowed on the new windward side
Heading	Magnetic bearing of direction of boat

Kicker	Control pulling or pushing boom downwards (vang)
Kite	Spinnaker or gennaker
Kiwi (gybe drop)	The gybe and spinnaker drop are performaed simultaneously with the sail stowed on the new windward side
Layline	Upwind or downwind line to a mark, at optimum sailing angle
Lee bow tack	Aggressive tack ahead and to leeward of another beating boat
Leeward	The downwind side
Leverage	Distance from another beating boat, measured perpendicular to the wind direction
Line of equality	Theoretical line at right angles to wind direction to compare positions
Loose cover	Sailing upwind and on the same tack as another boat while avoiding slowing it with one's wind shadow
Lubber lines	Lines marked on compass
Luffing	Altering course toward the wind
OCS	On course side of the start line (before the starting signal)
Oscillating shifts	Wind shifts back and forth around a mean
Overstanding	Sailing beyond the layline
Permanent shift	Wind permanently changes direction
Persistent shift	Wind shifts persistently in one direction
Pressure	Wind speed
PRO	Principal race officer

Glossary

Reach	Sailing direction between beating and running	Veered wind	Wind direction has moved clockwise
Rhumb line	Direct line between marks	Velocity header	Tacking angle/ instantaneous apparent wind angle changing with wind speed
Run	Sailing with the wind behind		
Sailing wind	The wind felt in tide or current, by any boat not anchored or moored	VMG (velocity made good)	Speed made toward or away from the wind, rather than speed through water
Shift, left	Wind direction has moved anticlockwise	Waving	Calling a give way boat past
Shift, right	Wind direction has moved clockwise	Wiggle	Tactical manoeuvre to break an overlap
Shift line	Layline created when wind shifts	Wind bend	Wind direction affected by local topography
Slam dunk	Tacking to close cover another boat which is ducking	Wind breaks	Wind strength affected by obstructions
Soaking	Downwind: sailing as close as possible to a dead run	Windward	Toward the direction the wind is blowing from
Split tacks	Sailing on opposite tacks to a second boat to determine the favoured side of the beat	Wipe off	Using other boats or obstructions to drop covering boat
Start line bias	Angle at which line differs from being square to wind		
Swinging oscillating shifts	Wind shifts progressively back and forth around a mean		
Tacking angle	Angle between port tack/starboard tack close hauled		
Tide	Cyclical current		
Transit	Position judged by lining up two objects		
Transom	Back of boat		
True wind direction (TWD)	Compass bearing from which wind is blowing		
Vang	See kicking strap/kicker		

Index

Index

Index